# THREE BOY SCOUTS
# IN AFRICA

## On Safari with Martin Johnson

BY

ROBERT DICK DOUGLAS, Jr.
DAVID R. MARTIN, Jr.
DOUGLAS L. OLIVER

*Illustrated*

G. P. PUTNAM'S SONS
NEW YORK — LONDON
The Knickerbocker Press
1928

THREE BOY SCOUTS IN AFRICA

The
Knickerbocker
Press
New York

To

OSA JOHNSON AND MARTIN JOHNSON

OUR GENEROUS AFRICAN HOSTS

# PREFACE

I HAVE just been reading through the fascinating book which Dave, Doug and Dick have made from their diaries of a six weeks' *safari* with the Martin Johnsons. It is a fine climax to one of the most romantic adventures the Scout Movement has been able to offer its younger members.

*Three Boy Scouts in Africa!* Africa is in a sense the home of the Scout Movement. Sir Robert Baden-Powell thought out and tried many of his ideas there, and learned much from the hundreds of Scouts who were drawn to Africa from all over the world, thirty and forty years ago, as the last place left where they could practice their pioneering craft. Tanganyika is one of the few wild game haunts in the world, and the spell of both Scout and unspoiled wilderness is in this book.

Perhaps it would be fitting to make a record here of the development of this plan for sending three Boy Scouts on *safari* with Martin Johnson. At the Annual Meeting of the National Council of the Boy Scouts of America in May, 1927, in New York, at the suggestion of Col. Theodore Roosevelt a new rank to be known as Honorary Scout was created. To its membership would be eligible only American citizens, those men, conspicuous for their attainments in exploration, and worthwhile outdoor adventure, who were regarded as heroes by our boys. Among the eighteen men appointed to this new and exclusive rank in Scouting was George Palmer Putnam, famous for his own expeditions to the North in the "Morrissey." On these expeditions he had always taken some boys, including his son David, who, as a boy of twelve, had accompanied William Beebe in the "Arcturus" expedition. Not only had Mr. Putnam succeeded in opening up a whole field of boy adventure by this means, but the simple narratives written by these and other boys when published had been read eagerly. His new interest in the Boy Scout Movement led him to suggest that the Boy Scout Movement send as the guests of himself and his son David, two boys chosen from its membership for a summer *safari* with Mr. and Mrs. Martin Johnson in the wild game country of Africa. (Another boy was added later through the generosity of Mr. David T. Layman, Jr.)

# PREFACE

In accepting this offer the Boy Scouts of America were particularly happy that it would be under the guidance of Mr. and Mrs. Johnson, whose wonderful work in big game photography, and whose genuine love and interest in the wild life of Africa, were so closely allied in spirit to its own attitude. Even of the lion, which so many Afrikanders regard as a pest to be exterminated at every opportunity, they spoke with real sympathy and admiration.

The three boys chosen for this expedition represented the entire membership of over 600,000 boys. Every Local Council was invited to make recommendations on the basis of outdoor experience, good Scouting and ability to write. Over 200 councils submitted candidates specially qualified and representing their choice within their membership. A very careful preliminary elimination was made by a committee of four members and checked by another four. The 17 candidates standing at the head of the list were submitted to another committee and seven of their number were chosen to appear personally before a committee consisting of Col. Theodore Roosevelt, Mr. Putnam and myself. From this number, David Martin, Douglas Oliver and Dick Douglas were chosen.

Three independent groups rated them first, the boys chosen being the preference of the seven final candidates themselves.

I cannot resist expressing my satisfaction here with the outcome of the entire expedition. From beginning to end it has moved without the slightest hitch. The boys have not known a day's illness. Of even greater satisfaction is the manner in which these boys have played their part. On two matters we knew that the expedition would be a test of the value of Scout training. What effect would the nation-wide publicity have on these boys? was one of the questions we asked ourselves. I am happy to say that they came back from Africa just as clean and wholesome and unspoiled as they were when they first came into my office to present themselves for personal examination before the committee that chose them from the seven final candidates.

The Sixth Scout Law declares that a Scout is a friend of animals, that he will not hurt or kill any living creature needlessly, that he will strive to save and protect all harmless life. It was inevitable that there would be some shooting on the *safari*. Fifty to a hundred native boys had to be fed. I refrained purposely from giving them any specific advice in this matter, and I find a great deal of satisfaction in the manner in which they worked out their own attitude and responsibility.

I congratulate our Three Boy Scouts on the book they have written, and I apologize to my boy reader for keeping him so long from the boys' narrative of their own adventure.

JAMES E. WEST,
Chief Scout Executive.

# FOREWORD

WHEN Doug and Dick and Dave sailed for Africa, I certainly wanted to go. Any American boy would. And when they got back, and I heard of their wonderful experiences, I wished more than ever that I too had had a safari with Mr. and Mrs. Martin Johnson.

However, the next best thing to making a safari one's self is a chance to read about it. I like this book *Three Boy Scouts in Africa* a lot. And it seems to me that most everyone interested in out-of-doors, and adventures, and the things that boys enjoy, will like it too. It certainly is very real and very interesting.

*David Binney Putnam*

# PUBLISHERS' NOTE

JUST as this book goes to press a letter, evidently delayed in transmission, reached the Chief Executive of the Boy Scouts, from Martin Johnson. In part it reads as follows:

Nairobi, British East Africa
August 18, 1928

DEAR MR. WEST:

As it now stands, the boys leave here for home at four o'clock this afternoon.

I feel certain that no one ever had a better or more exciting or more successful safari than we have just finished. Certainly no human being of modern times ever saw more game—for it can't be done. They actually saw millions of animals: about two hundred lions, leopards, cervil cats, gennet cats, many cheeta, hundreds of hyena, several herds of buffalo, thousands of giraffe, tens of thousands of Tommies, Granties, topi, kongoni, impalla, dik-dik, steinbuck, bushbuck, reedbuck, waterbuck, orabi, etc., and actually millions of zebra and wildebeest.

## PUBLISHERS' NOTE

No one ever saw lions at closer quarters. We have taken the boys to within thirty feet of lions at many times, and we have had exciting adventures —especially at night while making flashlights. . . .

Mrs. Johnson and I have had a wonderful time in the past five weeks in showing the boys the wonders of Tanganyika, and now we hate to let them leave. Three more polite, clean and clear thinking boys could not have been sent. They have helped the Boy Scout Movement in this country, and have left a fine impression of the real American boy.

Sincerely yours,

MARTIN JOHNSON.

# CONTENTS

# ILLUSTRATIONS

(From Photographs by Martin Johnson and the Three Boy Scouts)

xvii

# ILLUSTRATIONS

# ILLUSTRATIONS

# ILLUSTRATIONS

# INTRODUCTORY CHAPTER

SURELY we were the three happiest Scouts in America! We had just learned that we were chosen to spend the summer with the Martin Johnsons and accompany them on an African "safari" or caravan. As Mr. and Mrs. Johnson had just spent nine years in Africa making moving pictures of big game and nearly every other animal in Africa, and after having seen their famous lion picture, *Simba*, we knew that a summer spent with them would be an experience that we should remember all our lives.

Many boys have read the books by David Binney Putnam about his trips to the Arctic with his father, and to the Equator with William Beebe. It was the remarkable success of these books written by a boy that gave Mr. Putnam the idea of giving a similar chance to two Boy Scouts.

The offer first appeared in *Boys' Life* under the title, "How would you like to go to Africa?" Then details of the competition were given. Each local council was asked to select one or two of its members. This selection made, each scout sent in his application. This consisted of his rank and record in Scouting, his scholastic record, letters of recommendation, and a number of themes and essays written by him. This last was to show the writing ability of the scout, for those selected were to write a book about their trip.

From this number, seven were chosen. These reported to New York for further personal examination by a committee consisting of Chief Scout Executive James E. West, Col. Theodore Roosevelt, and Mr. Putnam. At first two scouts were to go as the guests of Mr. Putnam and David; but then it was announced that Mr. David T. Layman of New York had offered to make it possible for three to go. However, not until after the seven scouts had returned home did we learn the final selection.

Dave's family heard of his good fortune before he did. He had stopped for two days with his scoutmaster and son in Chicago. The telegram reached his home while he was on his way. As the news had at once been published in the papers, every one in Austin knew of Dave's selection before he arrived.

Dick was in school when word came that he

was to make the trip to Africa. At the moment all the school was in the assembly hall for a regular program. When Dick's father telephoned to the school the Principal read the telegram before the assembly. Of course Dick was pushed forward and had to say something, but he was too happy to say much.

Doug was down at the telegraph office when his telegram came. He knew that no matter who was selected, messages would be sent to every one of the seven scouts. As Mr. West had told us that the telegram would be sent on the Monday after we left New York, Doug was waiting for the news. When he heard of his selection he ran first to scout headquarters, then home to tell his folks the good news.

About a week later we got a telegram from National Headquarters telling us to report in New York on June 4th. From then until the time we left home we could think and talk of nothing but our African safari with the Martin Johnsons. We read everything we could find and looked up all the maps of East Africa. Martin Johnson's own book, then just published, *Safari*, naturally interested us most—it gives a wonderful picture of Africa. Dave even hunted all over town for a book on the native languages.

Of course all our friends asked us to bring back elephant skins, rhino ears, and leopard hides. Tigers were also in demand, although there has never been a tiger in Africa.

In New York our equipment was got together at the Boy Scout Trading Post. This is a unique store, made to look as nearly as possible like an old trading post on the western frontier. Instead of the regular furniture of an ordinary shop, all the fittings are made of hickory in its natural state, with the bark still on the wood. Even the walls are covered with logs, making it appear to be the stockade around the post.

On the first night we went around to see Mr. Layman. After dinner we enjoyed a very good mystery play called *The Silent House*.

One of the most interesting things we saw while in New York was a patrol of scouts in New Rochelle. We went out there to spend the night in Mr. West's beautiful home. After dinner the patrol came around to see us. It is called the Service Patrol and is composed of Eagle scouts from the various troops of the city. It is formed for the purpose of serving the community. We were pleasantly surprised when the boys presented us all with fine leather wallets made by themselves.

On the way back from Mr. West's home, we stopped at the Bronx Zoo, there meeting Mr. Ditmars, the famous authority on snakes, who conducted us through the park. He showed us practically all the animals which we were likely to meet in Africa.

Then we spent a night at the home of Colonel Roosevelt at Oyster Bay. The Colonel took us up to Sagamore Hill, the home of his father, the late president. We met the president's widow who showed us the family collection of hunting trophies, war souvenirs, and books given her husband by famous people. Colonel Roosevelt, by the way, is an honorary Scout, as is Mr. Putnam also.

The day before leaving New York, we had lunch on the *Ile de France*, the fine French Line ship on which we were to sail. There were Barron Collier and George Pratt, Colonel Roosevelt, of the Scout Executive Board, Mr. West, Mr. Putnam, "Scotty" Allan, Corey Ford, George Cherry, Dr. Fisher, Fitzhugh Green, and several others. We met for the first time David Putnam, just back from school.

The last night in New York, we spent at the home of Mr. Putnam. We were very much interested in David Putnam's museum of curios which he brought back from his trips to the Equator and to the Arctic. After dinner, we discussed with Mr. Putnam and David the problems involved in the writing of a book. Most of the next day we spent in last minute packing.

It is impossible to list here all the gifts and kindnesses which were showered upon us. For instance, the French Line made us their guests for the trip; their generous officials not only provided our passage to Europe and back, but saw that the Captain and officers of our ship knew that we were aboard. As a result we felt that we had pleasures and privileges far beyond the average passenger. From Marseilles to Mombasa and back we were generously treated by the Messagerie Maritimes, the steamship company, and throughout found many friends who helped us.

# THREE BOY SCOUTS IN AFRICA

# THREE BOY SCOUTS IN AFRICA

## CHAPTER I

### OFF AT LAST!

THE great moment of which we had been dreaming had come: we were off to Africa.

We boarded the *Ile de France* on the evening of June 9th, about nine-thirty after a small farewell dinner in New York. Several of our friends from National Headquarters came down to see us off. After all the good-byes and farewells had been said, the ship finally left her dock at about 12:30 A.M. and started down the Hudson River. We stayed up on the deck until the bright lights of lower New York had been passed and the Statue of Liberty was fading away on our right, then went down to our cabin and to bed.

Captain Blancart of the *Ile de France* was very

3

kind in taking us up on the bridge and explaining the use of the different instruments used in the navigation of the ship. Contrary to custom, the Captain allowed us free run of the bridge.

The whole voyage was pleasant and the weather perfect with the exception of the last day out when the sea became a little rough. Dave and Dick were slightly seasick. At least they said so; though a person who doesn't think of anything but food can't be very ill! On the way over we spent most of the time playing deck tennis, shuffle board, and other deck games. We also enjoyed the use of the gymnasium. We had a lot of fun being with "Bill" Tilden, the great tennis player, who was most awfully nice to us.

We landed in Havre on Friday morning. On Thursday afternoon the ship stopped in Plymouth harbor to let off those who were going to England. When we arrived in Havre on Friday morning the scouts of that city met us on the boat. They presented us with flowers and candy. After exchanging greetings we boarded the train for Paris.

The trip from Havre to Paris was very interesting. The first part was through hillsides on which we saw gardens hanging almost vertically.

4

DAVE, DOUG AND DICK.

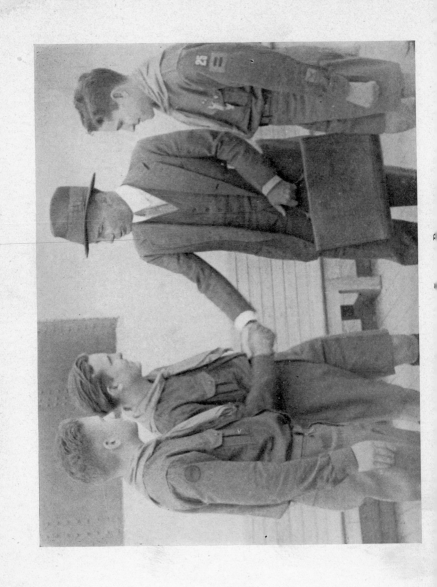

# OFF AT LAST!

Most of the houses were made of concrete with roofs of slate, although many had roofs of thatched grass with flowers growing on them. Then the country widened out into meadows, stretching on each side of the Seine River. Now and then, we passed little villages; no stores or large buildings, only a group of houses with a stone church and perhaps an inn or two.

When we arrived in Paris, we met a group of French scouts at the station. The national scout commissioner of the Eclaireurs Unionistes, M. Guerin Des-Jardins, was also there.

The boy scouts of France are divided into three separate groups, all working together but under no one head. There are the Eclaireurs Union-istes, who are connected with the Y. M. C. A., the Scouts de France, who are the Catholic Scouts, and the Eclaireurs de France, composed of those Protestants not in the first group. The leaders of the Scout movement in France are working toward an organization united and under one head similar to our own movement.

M. Guerin Des-Jardins took us to the Hotel Astoria which was to be our home for five days. Later an official of the always-thoughtful French Line took us to visit the Louvre, one of the largest art museums in the world. We spent

5

all the afternoon walking through the museum and looking at things of interest.

We were especially interested in the collection of ship models which Louis XIV had ordered to have made. Among the ships were models of every type of vessel up until the time of his death. Since then, models of modern ships have been added to the collection until the groups are complete in every detail.

After some six hours in the Louvre, we went to Notre Dame. It is on a little island in the center of Paris. This sounds strange, but the River Seine actually does make an island. It was here that Paris was first started many centuries ago. The windows of Notre Dame are all of stained glass with beautiful colors and designs.

After we had seen the cathedral we went back to the hotel. It is on the Avenue de Champs-Elysées and is only one block from the Arc de Triomphe. Soldiers returning from the war marched through the Arc de Triomphe and down the Champs-Elysées. Half way down the avenue is a large monument. It is a single block of reddish stone and called Cleopatra's Needle. It was brought to France from Egypt by Napoleon. The Champs-Elysées extends from

the Arc de Triomphe at one end to the Louvre at
the other.

That evening when we wanted to have some
clothes washed Doug rang the bell for the maid.
She came in rattling French at a great rate. As
none of us spoke any French we didn't know
what she was talking about. Dave handed her
a pair of his pajamas. She took them, looked
puzzled, then carefully folded them and handed
them back.

Dick now took the pajamas and went through
all the motions of washing and hanging out to
dry. All at once the maid understood. She
laughed and took all the clothes. Just as she
started out we happened to think that maybe
the laundry would not get back in time since
we had to leave in three days.

We all started telling her that we wanted the
laundry back on the second. Of course, we
could not make her understand.

Doug had a bright idea. He went over to
the clock on the wall and ran his finger around
it four times for forty-eight hours. The maid
nodded her head in understanding and, taking a
key from her pocket, she wound up the clock!

Finally we gave up and rang for the valet who
spoke English. When he interpreted for us the

7

maid explained that our clothes would be back the next night.

We went to the Eiffel Tower, the tallest structure ever built. We took the elevator to the top which is nine hundred and eighty-four feet from the ground. We easily believed this as the elevator climbed higher and higher. The top of the shaft never seemed to get any closer. When we looked over the side of the car the people got smaller and smaller. Dick said, "Those people down there look like ants." Then Dave made a wise crack with, "Look over by those trees. That's no ant. That's an uncle!" By the time we stopped laughing we had reached the top. We spent almost an hour up there in the sky looking over Paris. It was interesting to try to pick out the different buildings we had visited. There is a wonderful view from the platform on the top. As Dick said, it's an "Eyefull Tower."

The next day we visited the headquarters of the Sea Scout troop of Paris, a boat moored in the Seine River. While we were there we enjoyed very much a lunch cooked and served by the boys themselves.

After lunch we crossed from the boat to the bank. There were both a gang plank and a rope to use. As the French scouts came across on the rope we followed them. Doug and Dick got across safely but Dave lost his hold and, letting out a yell, fell into the water up to his waist.

Now we went out to the Château de Sillery where we attended a rally of Scouts and witnessed an initiation of some Wolf Cubs. These were boys too young to be Scouts. Their organization is affiliated with the scouts, however, and the boys pass straight from its ranks into scouting. While we were there we had the privilege of meeting Marshal Foch who is very much interested in French Scouting.

In Paris, we were honored by meeting Ambassador Herrick. With him, we met Mortimer Schiff, vice-president of the Boy Scouts of America. From the Ambassador's home we went to the tomb of the Unknown Soldier, on which we placed a wreath of flowers. Later, when we returned to Paris we met Gene Tunney.

When "Lindy" flew across the Atlantic, he landed at Le Bourget Field in Paris, one of the most important terminals for flying throughout Europe. We drove out to the field and saw the tablet marking the spot of his landing. An average of forty passenger planes leave the field each day.

We spent almost a whole day out at Versailles. On our way out we stopped at the castle which was the home of Josephine, Napoleon I's wife. It has since been made into a museum. Many famous documents issued by Napoleon are there; also many of his medals, swords, clothes, and other personal belongings. We then went on to Versailles and had lunch in a small café on the grounds.

We went back to our hotel, having had one of the most interesting days spent in Paris. We were glad to find that our clothes were back from the laundry. Going over the bill we found one item marked "lady's pajamas—10 francs." We were puzzled for a minute and then remembered that Dave's pajamas, although regular men's pajamas, had a lot of fancy trimmings. The woman at the laundry had naturally mistaken them for lady's pajamas. We kidded him about this for several days.

# CHAPTER II

## THROUGH THE SUEZ

NEXT morning we began the second stage of our trip. At 9:00 A.M. we boarded the train for Marseilles. Mr. Durand of the French Line kindly accompanied us; when we returned, he took care of us again. Late in the afternoon we got a glimpse of the snowy Alps.

Late that night we arrived in Marseilles. Once more a group of scouts was at the station to meet us. Next morning we took a trip to the Château d'If, which is built on a little island in the Mediterranean about a mile from shore. This was one of the great prisons of the French Revolution. The "Man with the Iron Mask," Louis Phillipe, and many other famous men of France were imprisoned here. The story, *The Count of Monte Cristo*, was written about this terrible place. After three hours wandering about the château we went back to the shore and had a good lunch in a little café overlooking the

Mediterranean Sea. After lunch we went to the pier where the *S.S. Dumbea* of the Messagerie Maritime Line was docked. She was to be our home for the next three weeks. The first thing we noticed was how small she was; only about one-fifth the size of the *Ile de France*, having a displacement of ten thousand tons.

On the *Dumbea* we were to meet many interesting people; some from Madagascar, others returning home from visiting Europe, military officials, and many who had been everywhere and seen all the sights of the world.

As the Mediterranean turned out to be very smooth, the trip to Port Said was the most pleasant of our whole voyage. We passed through the strait between Corsica and Sardinia, and later, the Straits of Messina which separate Sicily from Italy.

Five days after embarking we landed at Port Said. In this city there seemed to be people of every nation on earth. All languages we ever heard of were being spoken; and any kind of money was accepted by the shop keepers. When we landed, we were besieged by persistent peddlers selling everything from cigarettes to postcards. These fellows follow the traveller for blocks.

SHOOTING THE SUN ON THE BRIDGE OF THE *Ile de France*.

On the Battlefields of France.

One of the interesting sights was a "gila-gila" man performing his tricks, making two chickens from one, making coins disappear, and other examples of the conjurer's art.

Port Said is at the northern end of the Suez Canal. All ships passing through the canal must stop here; therefore it is a very important port. We were told that the town attracted many thieves and scoundrels as well as honest people.

After leaving Port Said we entered the Suez Canal. It took fourteen hours to pass through. At the start it was mainly a man-made ditch, just a wide avenue of water with stone walls. Half-way down the canal there were several lakes, then more of the actual canal. On either side spreads a wide expanse of desert backed by distant mountains. At the southern end lies Suez, a town of forty thousand people.

We next entered the Gulf of Suez. It is about one hundred and fifty miles long and is bordered by deserts on one side and mountains on the other.

The Gulf of Suez and the Red Sea are rich in traditions contained in ancient Biblical History. At one time we could see Mount Sinai dimly outlined on the horizon; while at another time we passed over the spot where Moses and the Children of Israel crossed during their flight from Egypt.

From the Gulf of Suez we entered the Red Sea where we spent four days of terrible heat. Rays of the sun were so strong that we were compelled to wear pitch helmets even under two thicknesses of canvas which covered the boat. The air was so filled with moisture that the perspiration did not evaporate from our bodies. We spent the time lolling in the shade. Nearly everyone slept on deck.

Three days out we were hailed by a small dhow, or native boat. The *Dumbea* stopped and learned that the few natives and the Arab owner aboard her had been without food and water for over two days. We stocked them up and proceeded on our course to Djibouti.

Upon arriving at Djibouti on Sunday July 1st, we saw several natives swimming out to meet us.

They called, "*Monsieur, Monsieur, A la mer, A la mer.*" (meaning mister, mister, into the sea, into the sea).

They wanted passengers to throw coins into the water. Several did and the native boys proceeded to dive for them.

American Scouts would be envious if they

could have seen these natives swim and dive. Some of the boys, for a shilling, would even swim under the ship. To do this they had to go down about twenty-five feet.

We went ashore and had a walk around the town. Djibouti was more our idea of an eastern port than Port Said. Nearly all the inhabitants were black. The poorer class lived in grass huts surrounding the town, while the better ones lived in plaster houses. There are many afflicted people here. In fact, we found it depressing to see many with hardly any legs and others with arms as thin as broomsticks. Half the people seemed to make their living by begging from the tourists and the other half from selling fake curios consisting of "genuine Abyssinian Knives" (usually made in Germany) and hand woven shawls (made in some northern textile mill.)

While at Djibouti we saw a native dance with weird chanting and strange steps which was all very interesting. We had just turned a corner when we came upon a large crowd of natives following five or six dancers. The latter wore enormous headdresses of feathers and grass, and their bodies were painted in many colors. They carried native harps and tom-toms. To our surprise, our guide told us that it was a funeral procession for a boy who had died the day before. Doug tried to get some moving pictures but the crowd was gone before he was ready.

Glad to be free from the filth and stench of Djibouti we proceeded through the Gulf of Aden, around Cape Guardafui and into the Indian Ocean where we encountered high winds and large waves.

The day after passing Guardafui our cabin was flooded. Dave had just put on some clean clothes and was standing before the open port hole when a big wave hit the side of the boat and came splashing into the room. Everything was soaked including Dave. Luckily we had most of our clothes inside our suit cases and water-proof duffle bags, but all our bedding was soaked. We laughed at Dave when he came up on deck; but felt different when we saw the cabin.

From Guardafui to Mombasa, a trip of six days, we saw no land. The only life around was the hundreds of flying fish, which leaped out of the water, flying for about twenty yards and diving in again. We also saw one or two sharks and a few porpoises.

SHUFFLEBOARD ON THE *Ile de France.*

THE BOYS MEET GENE TUNNEY IN PARIS.

# CHAPTER III

## WE REACH AFRICA

AFTER a night of wild dreams, we awoke and dressed. Looking through the porthole, we saw land. This land meant more to us than just the fact that it was solid earth. It stood for Martin Johnson, lions, adventure, and just about everything that sounds good to a boy.

We soon steamed into the Kilindini harbor of Mombasa. The town of Mombasa is on an island just off the coast of Kenya, or British East Africa. As Mombasa harbor is too small to permit large ships to enter, they anchor in Kilindini harbor, on the other side of the island. Kilindini is one of the deepest harbors in the world, the name itself meaning "deep water."

After the doctors, police, and other officials had finished, we were allowed to go ashore. We were about to leave in a row boat, when two boy scouts hailed us from a motor boat. Gosh, we were glad to see them! They were Herbert

Wright and Bill Rainbow, of Nairobi, who had come to help us with our baggage. With them was Mrs. Bulkley, wife of the Mombasa Port Manager. The District Commissioner also met us and took us through the customs house. When Dave had to pay a good deal of money for bringing in his trumpet he began to wish he had left it at home. Dick and Doug kidded him and said, "I told you so."

After the immigration and customs officers got through with us, we drove out to the home of Mrs. Bulkley where we had lunch. As it was the first meal that approached an American set-up since leaving home, we all enjoyed it to the limit. It surely was good to taste home-made white bread and fresh vegetables.

After lunch, Mrs. Bulkley drove us around Mombasa. We saw the native quarter, the bazaar, and the camel camp. Here the camels grind oil from the seeds of one of the native trees. The hard matter left after the oil has been pressed out is then fed to the animals. As they walk round and round, turning the mill, the camels are blindfolded.

Mrs. Bulkley and the two scouts arranged for us to see the prison which lies right on the water-front. It was once a Portuguese fort, being at least three hundred and fifty years old. The Arabs captured it after a long siege. Then later the British took it. When the fort was made into a prison it was connected to another small outpost a mile away by a long tunnel cut through solid rock.

A few weeks before we had arrived at Mombasa a native superstition had come true. The superstition was that if an old Arabic vase standing on a shelf among the ruins of an ancient tower were ever broken the person who broke it would drop dead. A native boy had seen the vase when he was hunting and had shot an arrow at it. The vase broke and the boy at once fell dead. Now no natives will touch the broken parts with the exception of a Mohammedan priest.

Boarding the Kenya and Uganda railway, we started the twenty-hour trip to Nairobi. Our way was mainly through small towns and up steep grades. In fact we climbed five thousand feet in a little over three hundred miles.

After messing ourselves up by eating mangos, —we turned in.

When I awoke the country along the road was very different from that we had seen the night before. Instead of mountains, we were now surrounded by a flat country covered with bushes and scrubby trees. At once we began to look for the game; but it was some time before we saw any. The first thing we saw was a cheetah. This is a member of the cat family, and is about the size of a small leopard. The cheetah can run very fast, and in a different manner from that of the lion and the leopard, which stalk their prey. The cheetah runs down his victims, being able to outdistance any of the antelopes or gazelle for a short run. We saw this fellow over on a hillside, sitting on his haunches and staring at the train.

Just about this time, Bill Rainbow, the African Boy Scout with us, got into an argument with one of the porters on the train. Bill wanted to throw banana peelings out of the window while the porter wanted to close the window. Bill jabbered at the porter all the time in Swahili, the common language which almost all the natives understand. Pretty soon he began to throw the peels at the porter who got so tickled that he started laughing. Finally he shook so hard that he couldn't close the window at all, but just stood there while Bill threw bananas at his face. That black fellow certainly had a great sense of humor.

Soon we began to see bunches of wildebeest, hartebeest, or kongoni, Thompson's gazelle (called "Tommies" for short), and Grant's gazelle. Now and then, a few ostriches went striding across the veldt, as the people call the flat, grassy plain that makes up most of Kenya and Tanganyika.

Just before lunch time the train pulled into Nairobi. As it slowed down at the station the first person we saw as we looked out the window was Mr. Martin Johnson. Though he was dressed in regular civilian clothes, we all instantly recognized him from seeing his pictures both in his book *Safari* and in the moving picture, *Simba*. He is a big fine looking man, very powerfully built and full of energy. Then we saw Mrs. Johnson, whom we liked at once. At the train to meet us were also Mr. and Mrs. Gilfillan, American friends of the Johnsons; and Mr. Caldwell, the game warden of Kenya.

"Well, I was expecting something quite different!"

That was Mr. Johnson's greeting. Then he explained that the cablegram from Mr. Putnam announcing our arrival said "sending three fine dogs." That's what a local telegraph operator did with the word "boys," which he had changed to "dogs."

We went right out about three miles to the home of the Johnsons. After a pleasant lunch we drove into town to get a few things we needed for safari.

After dinner, we spent some time packing, transferring our clothes from our suitcases to the metal safari boxes which we were to take. All of us turned in early; but lots of good it did! None of us could sleep a wink for thinking of tomorrow's safari.

That day we made our first progress in our Swahili. The words we learned were *"Chukula T'harri,"* or "food is ready."

# CHAPTER IV

## INTO THE WILDERNESS

ON the morning of July 11th we prepared for an early start. We were certainly excited! We could hardly wait to get off "into the blue," as they call the open spaces in Africa.

We stayed in town for two hours for some final shopping and then went home. (We had already learned to call it "home" due to the Johnsons' wonderful hospitality.) Meanwhile, two big lorries, a Federal Knight and a Chevrolet truck, loaded with supplies left for Tanganyika. Nine native boys went in the trucks with Kima, the little pet monkey of the Johnsons. The latter, by the way, was very much displeased with the motorcar and her box.

Shortly afterward, Mr. and Mrs. Johnson and we three followed in the Willys-Knight touring car. Dick and Dave rode in the back of the car on boxes covered with blankets. They thought

23

their seats were just like a king's throne until we started to hit bumps. Then they sadly found out different; for first they would hit the top, then bounce back on to the boxes. Before we had gone many miles, they were black and blue and yelling for mercy.

Our course took us among hills surrounding, beautiful velvety green valleys and plains. Next the road led through the great Rift Valley probably the greatest valley in the world. It extends from Southern Arabia through the entire length of Africa. Scientists say that it was the last part of Africa which was covered by water. Shells may be found if one digs a few feet into the earth. Though the bottom of the valley is about two thousand feet above sea level, the mountains surrounding it are over five thousand feet high. The section of the Rift Valley through which we were passing was called "The Kedong."

The road wound down through the hills to the bottom of the valley, then across it and up the other side. It was in the valley that we first began to see game. There were herds of wildebeest, kongoni, Tommies (Thompson's gazelle) and zebra. We had seen the others before; but this was our first sight of zebra.

Tommies seem to be perhaps the happiest animals in Africa. You never see one of them but what its little tail is wagging. We saw one which had a very sore leg and was limping; but he seemed as happy as ever. His tail was wagging and his head nodding as usual. Tommies are also very pretty animals, having a black stripe running down each side, and pure white stomachs. Their backs are a very light brown.

Suddenly Mr. Johnson said, "I'll bet a shilling that we see giraffe in ten minutes."

Sure enough, in ten minutes we did see giraffe, a whole herd of about fifteen. They were queer looking creatures as they stood under, or rather among, the flat topped trees. Their yellow and black bodies showed against the tree trunks while their long necks ran up among the foliage and their queer heads with little stumpy horns stuck clear up above the trees.

As we drove along we saw vultures swinging in circles through the air. At first we thought it was a lion kill (an animal of some kind which has been killed by a lion); because when a lion makes a kill and is eating it the vultures hover over him until he is through, when they drop down and eat what is left. We found, however, that it was a zebra killed by a white man for its skin. All over Kenya and Tanganyika are white men who kill zebra for hides. They get about two dollars and a half for each skin. One man has been known to slaughter as many as three hundred in one day, Mr. Johnson told us.

After the giraffe and zebra we saw no more game that day. We went on until we reached a little river where we stopped for the night. We three at once started out to gather wood and build a fire, just as any Boy Scouts would. But Mr. and Mrs. Johnson said to let the "boys" do it, meaning the natives. In a safari there are plenty of these "boys"; two or three personal servants, gun bearers, porters, and skinners. Of course, they are grown men.

When we went to set up our cots we were again told to "let the boys do it." In all our experiences on hikes and in Boy Scout camps back at home, we had always done most of the work. So it did not feel natural to stand around while the natives pitched camp. Doug said he didn't feel right because if he did not do something to keep in condition he would have an awful let-down when he reached home. But Dave and Dick both enjoyed it. They figured that it would probably be the only time in their lives when they had to do nothing at all.

Suka, or personal boy, even unpacked our safari boxes and got our pajamas. After a fine dinner, cooked by a native chef over a camp fire, we went to bed and slept soundly on our first night of actual safari.

We were pretty sleepy; but after this day of wonders we couldn't doze off without a last word about what wonderful folks the Johnsons had turned out to be. Out in the African blue they were just as real as any one could be, and certainly real friends to us. Indeed, how Mr. Johnson could put up with some of the crazy things we did and said, was a miracle.

We soon found out that Mr. Johnson's greatest interest is to preserve animals and their habitations for future generations, chiefly by making a record of both in film form.

But only half the credit should go to Mr. Johnson. Mrs. Johnson deserves the other half. She had been places where no white man except her husband has been. No hardships are too severe for her. She has been captured by cannibals, chased by rhino, buffalo, and elephant, marooned on several islands and has gone through scores of storms at sea. Among other

27

things, she is a fine shot, to say nothing of her being the best cook by far.

She tried to teach us something about shooting, but none of us qualified as cooks—even third class!

# CHAPTER V

## WE REACH THE BASE CAMP

WHEN we awoke it was cold; or so it felt. Probably it was just because we were in Africa, about one degree south of the equator where any weather that was not boiling hot felt cold. We were going to get up and go down to the cold river to wash. But when we got up we found our boys had filled gasoline cans with water, heated it in the fire, and brought it to the tents. We certainly felt like kings.

When we started out this morning, Dave and Dick got seats in the back of the car again. They thought they were lucky to be able to stretch out and sleep, but their ideas were quickly changed. The bumps were about a foot high and two feet apart. When Dick and Dave saw a bump coming they would catch hold of the top and, after going into the air, let themselves down easy. When they didn't see it coming, though, they either hit the top of the car or came down with a terrible whack on the floor. Usually they did both. They laughed so much that they did not mind it though.

Once Dave starts laughing he cannot stop. Then Dick gets a fit at watching him. Laughter is a medicine for almost anything, but this time the pair had an overdose of it.

All that day, we rode over hills, flat stretches covered mostly with thorn trees, until we reached the plains. We began to see numerous herds of game. Tommies were the most plentiful. They loved to race the car. As we drove along, one would suddenly dash across the road, then race alongside for a hundred yards to cross again. Sometimes they kept this up for half a mile. While their elders were running, the little ones bounded along on stiff legs, looking exactly like small balls of fur on strings.

We saw quite a bit of new game that we hadn't seen before. Mr. Johnson pointed out topi, a queer headed antelope with brown and iron-gray skins; impalla bounding up and down in the same spot whenever we blew the horn or made some noise; a little bushbuck, which shot across the road so quickly that we hardly got a glimpse of his brown body; reedbuck, little brown fellows with short horns; and dik-dik, the smallest of all, not much larger than a rabbit.

Once when we stopped, Mrs. Johnson said we might begin to see lions in a short while. When we heard this we flipped a coin to see who would get the first one. For we had decided that while we would not shoot any other game, we would each try to get one lion.

Somehow, one doesn't feel the same about shooting a lion as about killing an innocent little Tommie, for instance. When one considers the amount of game lions kill each night and the cruelty with which they go about it, there is no self-reproach about shooting the murderer. The worst of it is that a lion often begins to eat its prey before the latter even dies. Mr. Johnson told us that he had found zebra still alive after having been partially devoured by a lion!

Mr. Johnson told us he was glad we didn't want to shoot any other game, but that as all the native boys he had must have food, some animals must be killed. He said that as long as such killing was unavoidable he saw no reason why we should not each select an animal with a good set of horns for a trophy. In this way, we might each get four or five good heads without killing any more than was necessary.

Doug won the toss for a shot at the first lion.

Dick and Dave said that they were glad not to get a shot first. They claimed their lion hunting had been sadly neglected and they were glad to see some one else try first!

At noon we had lunch in a native village where there was a very good garden. Mrs. Johnson bought some corn and fresh vegetables. We had corn on the cob for lunch. There was also a very good spring at the village. Mr. Johnson told us that he had often developed pictures here because the water was so clear.

From this village on for about fifty miles we were in the country of the Masai.

The Masai are a very "shenzi" or wild race of natives. They are the only tribe of natives that will not recognize the rule of the British government. Also they are among the richest in Africa since they raise much cattle, every head of which is valued at five dollars. Some of them who own very large herds are quite wealthy. As they never butcher their cattle the herds multiply by the hundreds.

Masai bleed their cattle by tying a string around the animal's neck, and then sticking a quill into the jugular vein. When enough blood has been taken from the animal they untie the string, and the wound soon heals.

Ambassador Herrick Greets the Scouts in Paris.

LOLLING IN THE HEAT OF THE RED SEA.

The blood so gotten is mixed with sour milk and kept in skin bottles. This mixture is the native's only food unless one of the cattle happens to die. In this case they eat the meat.

All afternoon we kept our eyes open for the sight of "simba," as the natives call a lion. We didn't see any, but we did see a cheetah, which also belongs to the cat family and is sometimes called the hunting leopard.

It got dark before we reached our destination. As we drove along with the head lights burning, there were eyes everywhere, innumerable pairs of tiny, red pin-points of light, staring at us from the blackness of the night. From their size we thought them to be Tommies. Night is a very tragic time for these little beasts, for it is then that their lives are so often snuffed out by carnivorous animals.

On finally arriving at camp we heard such a hullaballoo as we'd never heard before. The reason was that when the Johnsons came into Nairobi for us they had left most of their native boys at this base camp down in Tanganyika. As the boys are not allowed to shoot for fresh meat and their supply of "posho" (a native food made of ground-up corn) was running low, they were certainly glad when their "bwana" returned. As the car drove up it was immediately surrounded by boys yelling for joy.

As camp was all pitched we had nothing to do but eat and then go straight to bed. We were none too comfortable that night, for we'd learned that two cobras had been killed in camp the night before.

Next morning we had a chance to see the layout of camp. Dave and Doug were in one tent and Dick was in another. Each tent had a fly over it, the inside being the same as a wall tent. This fly made the tent a good shelter for the tropics; yet even with a double canvas over our heads we always had to wear our sun helmets between 9 A.M. and 5 P.M.

There was a still for making good drinking water out of the dirty water from the river which the boys brought to camp. When the water comes from the still it is as clear as crystal. The machine's average output is from five to ten gallons a day, and keeping the necessary fire burning beneath it requires all the time of one native boy.

Our storeroom was a native mud hut. All petrol (as the British call "gas") and oil, together with the skins, were kept in it. It was in this shelter that Bucari killed a cobra the night before.

The cook shack was the best place in camp. It was built out of grass. Pishie built his fire in front and did all his cooking there.

In our mess tent Mrs. Johnson took all the petrol boxes and made shelves out of them on which the food supplies were conveniently kept.

She had some of the chop boxes padlocked, and the contents rationed out because the boys often used too much of some staple or other.

One box she had especially to watch was the soap box. As the boys liked to watch the bubbles which soap made in the water, they used it whenever they could. Often a boy wasted a whole bar of laundry soap to wash a single shirt.

Around the camp was a path about ten feet wide from which all grass had been cut. This was a precaution in case of a fire on the plains.

All morning we helped get supplies put away and straighten the camp up a little.

# CHAPTER VI

## DOUG GETS HIS LION!

OUR first morning of actual safari began at
4:30 A.M., July 14th. The hyenas must
have known we were coming for they laughed all
night. Also two old lions had a nice duet a few
hundred yards from camp. They might have
been bemoaning the fact that their last zebra
was too tough, probably caused by running from
our motor cars! "Oh, for the good old days
when a lion could get at least a dozen zebra
without exertion!" they seemed to say.

Suka, our boy, (he claims he is fifty years old)
woke us. When he touched Doug he leaped
into the air—Doug, not Suka. Doug said he
had been dreaming of the two cobras which had
been killed in camp the day before.

The moon was still shining and all the stars
were out when we ate breakfast. It was still
dark when we left camp. We were armed with
three guns, a .470, .405 Winchester, and a

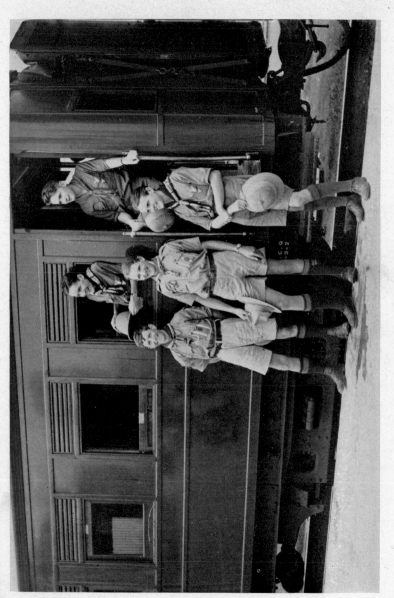

DICK, DOUG AND DAVE MEET THE AFRICAN SCOUTS.

MR. AND MRS. MARTIN JOHNSON.

Springfield army rifle. Mr. and Mrs. Johnson never go out without guns even though they are just after pictures.

Our chief aim was to get some pictures of lions and some meat for the boys. As meat spoils very quickly in the tropics it had to be secured every two or three days.

Lions are usually found in or near some "donga," meaning a ditch or gully. Whether it is a large deep ravine or just a tiny washout it is still a donga. We started out along one of the dongas near camp. As we had heard lions roaring up there the night before, Mr. Johnson thought this would be a good place to begin our search.

We had already learned that lions in Africa seldom roar as we heard them in a zoo. The sound they made in the open was a short grunting cough. This was to stampede the game, or to call other lions; or just in contentment after a good meal. They seemed very sly about roaring to stampede the game they are after. The intelligent lion puts his head down near the ground and then grunts loudly. The sound, travelling right above the earth, fooled the game who found it almost impossible to tell from the noise where a lion actually was. He might have been a mile away, two miles, or only a few hundred yards.

We had gone about a mile down the donga when Mrs. Johnson suddenly exclaimed, *"Simba!"*

*"Ndio,"* replied Bucari, the Nubian headman of the Johnsons. *Ndio* was Swahili for yes.

We immediately stopped and began to look up and down the donga for lions. For awhile we saw nothing. Then we got the thrill of our lives. Down in the tall grass were four big lions, the first wild lions we had ever seen. Three were females and the other was a young male.

We started up closer in hope of getting some pictures. But the beasts laid down in the grass and we couldn't get them.

We were not excited. Oh, no! What did four lions mean to us, particularly when they were only a few yards away? Of course we expected a charge. No doubt our hearts were beating a mile a minute.

But nothing happened. For a few minutes the lions simply watched us with a bored air. After awhile they all rose slowly and walked away, each giving us a look as if to say, "Gosh, what silly animals! I can't figure them out."

# DOUG GETS HIS LION!

As we were about to leave, Mrs. Johnson pointed out three more lions over a hill across the donga. They were beautiful creatures, slender and graceful as they lay in the shade of a tree. They really seemed much more like big tame cats than like wild African lions.

As we watched them a giraffe wandered down toward the donga. As soon as the lions saw him they flattened down in the grass. When the unsuspecting animal approached the lions we were sure that any minute he would be killed. But just before he reached the enemy the latter jumped up and ran away over the hill! We never knew whether we scared them or they just left, but we were glad the giraffe wasn't killed.

We came in a few minutes to a large stretch of veldt on which were grazing thousands of wildebeest, zebra, kongoni, Tommy, and a few topi and Grant's gazelle. The sight was a wonderful one. Originally, our conception of Africa was thick jungles full of snakes and monkeys or fever-ridden swamps. Here we were in a beautiful valley surrounded by miles of rolling plains, one of the healthiest spots on earth.

To the left of us were jackals and hyenas on a kill while a flock of vultures circled overhead,

waiting their turn to pick over the dead wildebeest. It was a sickening sight to see the
hyenas slinking away as we approached. Surely
the most righteous person on earth would like
to have taken a shot at these cowardly sneaks.

We were suddenly aware of a commotion
among the game. At once Mrs. Johnson pointed
out two lionesses stampeding some zebra.
When we went for them they saw us and ran
into a donga. We didn't pursue them because
it is very dangerous to follow game into high
grass. There is no telling what may spring out
at the hunter.

This year's big migration of the game ended
a few weeks before our arrival. What we saw
now was only a remnant. During the main
migration, Mr. Johnson told us there were millions of head of wildebeest and zebra. Their
coming was not unlike a great locust plague.
They left the plains behind them bare of grass.
At the time, lions did not stay among the main
body of the herd, but kept behind to prey on
the stragglers.

In the afternoon, we started out toward Lion
Valley. Very few of the places around camp had
names on the map, so Mr. and Mrs. Johnson
gave each some name. The first time they

were down in Tanganyika they discovered that this valley was almost always full of lions; hence the name.

When we first entered the valley we noticed the abundance of game. Zebra and wildebeest, the lion's chief food, were there in great numbers. The grass had been burnt off and recent rains had brought up the tender shoots of new grass, all of which brought the game. Following the game came the lions.

After going down the valley for a way we came to a waterhole. Here Mr. Johnson said he had almost always found lions. Scarcely were the words out of his mouth than we saw an old lioness down at the edge of a nearby donga. As we started toward her we saw four more on an ant hill; then four more on another. Before we got close the first four started away. Then we went up toward those on the other hill and got up within thirty or forty feet of them.

We had never seen a more beautiful sight in our lives. Lions have been pictured as terrible and aggressive; but they are like all other creatures when left alone. As long as we were not bothering they paid no more attention to us than to the birds in the trees overhead. They gave us a few dirty looks and let it go at that. After all of us had made some wonderful pictures, Mrs. Johnson made a roaring sound. To our surprise, instead of charging, the lions walked off to find a more peaceful resting place.

They walked around us and then up to the hill where the other four lions had been. They were not afraid of us, though this time they were just a bit cautious of the strange animals that they saw before them. They lay down on the ant-heap and watched us. Presently one of them rolled over on his side like a big cat and, after pawing at the air, went to sleep! We came over until we were only ten yards away and resumed our photographing. Surely it was one of the most beautiful sights we had ever seen, four big lions sprawled out on the hill watching us through half-closed eyes.

None of them had large manes. Very few of the wild lions do. Some of the biggest lions of Africa do not compare with circus lions in quality of mane. The lions living in the open get their manes full of burrs and thorns. Then they comb them out with their claws, often pulling out great bunches of hair. As the result of this the manes are usually short and not very thick.

We made pictures of them for about half an hour. They posed for us, standing, lying down, sitting on their haunches. As long as we remained there, they watched us. When we left we saw them, still on the hill, staring at us.

At that moment, foolish as it may sound, we all three hoped that the car would break down so that we would have to stay there all night. We could think of nothing more exciting than sleeping in trees with lions moving beneath us.

No sooner said than done: we had a puncture. There we were in the middle of the lion country with a punctured tire. However, by the time we changed tires we had thought better of the matter of camping there and were glad to move on.

It was not until an hour later that we saw the lion that was to play such a large part in our activities for the day. He was truly a "King of Beasts," a magnificent fellow with massive shoulders and long mane. Two lionesses followed him over the veldt into a donga. We hurried after to get a better sight of them. The big fellow was in a bad humor, that we could plainly see. But his curiosity proved stronger than his prudence. When he stopped for a look at us the two females ran away. As our chief business was with the old male, we gingerly approached the clump of grass in which he was hiding.

Mr. Johnson quickly set up his cameras to film the lion the minute he stuck his head out of the grass. He stuck his head out of the grass all right, but it was evident that he didn't want to be photographed.

Pretty soon he ran on to another clump of grass, then another. We chased him until his big muscle-bound body was tired out and his temper completely gone.

At last he was ready to charge. For a mark to shoot at, there was his head. It was a shot pretty hard to miss. Yet Doug was so excited he missed his first shot, the bullet going high.

In the second, the time spent in reloading, Doug must have felt as if the weight of the whole world was on his back. He aimed again for the angry lion's head and shot. This time the old fellow disappeared into the grass. Dick said that he had crawled through the donga. It was a scary moment.

Five minutes passed and we saw nothing of the lion. What we three thought during those five minutes would have kept us writing forever. Yet the lion might have still been living for all we knew, and charge us any second. Gosh, it

Our Cars Move Across the Serengetti Plains into Tanganyika.

"Now You're Getting Too All-Fired Close." He Growled and Lashed

was ticklish. As Mr. Johnson could not make out the complete form of the lion he went a little closer, much to our anxiety.

Just then Dave piped up with, "Think of poor Daniel."

We were in no mood for jokes, but we couldn't help laughing at that.

We waited about five minutes, then started slowly forward a few feet. We could see the lion on its side but could not tell if he were still alive. It was too dangerous to go in to the donga to see. A wounded animal is very much more dangerous than one not wounded, for he will charge at any person coming near him.

Mr. Johnson asked for something to throw. Dick told Dave to take off his shoe. He hesitated at first, afraid that the lion would chew it to pieces. Then he took it off and Mr. Johnson threw it at the lion. It hit with a thud and the lion did not move. At this, Mr. Johnson formally pronounced the big fellow dead. He measured about nine feet long from the head to the tip of the tail.

We now took the body back to camp. However, we had not yet obtained what we had set out for; namely, fresh meat for the boys. So Dick shot a topi. Bucari at once took out a large knife and "chingered," or bled the animal. This is the only condition under which the natives, who are Mohammedans, will eat meat. It is a part of the Mohammedan religion that unless meat has been bled and a prayer said while it is bleeding, it is not fit for food.

When the boys at camp saw Simba they all had a war dance. Ponda-ponda, Mr. Johnson's skinner, picked Doug up on his back and carried him all around camp. Mohammed, a porter, gave a war whoop and danced around while the Waccoma all joined in. Then the skinners got busy. After the skinner had finished this, he cut out the two lucky bones from the lion's shoulders.

In every member of the cat family there are two floating bones which are not connected to any other bones. These are supposed to bring the owner good luck. The natives made quite a ceremony of the presentation.

The skin of Doug's prize head was removed and salted. Then the flesh was scraped from the skull. Afterwards it was put into a tree to let the ants eat off all the bits of meat left. Mr. Johnson told us that each head would cost thirty or thirty-five dollars to be mounted. At that rate, we thought that we had better not save many heads. We might shoot for meat, but as for saving the heads to be mounted, it would break us.

When Dick first spoke of this we began kidding him about being a Scotchman. After that whenever Dick tried to save anything or keep anything, we always called him a Scotchman. Even when he licked pie plates, we said it was his Scotch blood. He remarked that he never saw much pie left on our plates, though.

That night for dinner, we had cocoanut pie. Mrs. Johnson said that whenever one of us got a lion, she would bake a pie for the one who shot it. There was quite an argument concerning the kind of pie. Doug wanted cocoanut, and Mr. Johnson wanted blueberry. But since Doug shot the lion his choice went.

# CHAPTER VII

## WE DEAL WITH NATIVES

TWO Waccoma natives came in during the night and told Mr. Johnson that the Masai were having lots of trouble with lions. Their story was that the natives were setting traps with spears to catch the marauders. In certain parts of the country, lions kill the cattle of the wandering tribes, thus destroying their food supply. Sometimes the beasts even carry off human beings.

We started across the veldt to visit this Masai tribe, crossing donga after donga on the way and passing a deserted Masai manyetta, or village. As the grass had apparently become too short for cattle the whole town moved on.

As the Masai roam about while their cattle graze they build only temporary camps or villages, surrounded by thorn bush fences to keep out lions, leopards and other dangerous animals. The young calves and sick cattle are kept inside

Mrs. Johnson and a Lion that Charged.

On the Way to Camp All Sorts of Game Ran Before Us.

the manyetta with the people. The natives use the manyetta as long as the grass lasts. All the time, the place is getting dirtier. The filth and stench is awful.

We saw no lions, but other game was plentiful. There were great herds of zebra which were like our American cow in one way: we never passed a herd, even though they were a long way off without their running across the road and stirring up so much dust that we could hardly see.

When we got to an inhabited manyetta many of the natives came filing out to meet us. They were all dressed up in what looked to be their war costumes. Their bodies were streaked with paint and large ornaments hung from their ears. Every one of them had his ears slit, and pieces of wood, bones or beads were hanging in the holes. All the men carried clubs and spears; and some of them had bows and arrows. It is said that the Masai put poison on the end of their arrows so that when a poison arrow hits an animal the animal is paralyzed.

They all shouted, "*Jambo! Jambo!*" as we approached. Now "jambo" might have meant anything on earth so far as our knowledge of the language went.

One particularly affable fellow stuck his hand

out to Dave and yelled, "*Jambo!*" Dave, much perplexed, answered, "I'm no circus elephant!" (We soon found out that "*jambo*" meant "hello.")

To gain their good will so that we could take some pictures, Doug handed out some little scout buttons. The natives promptly stuck them in their hair. Some of the warriors who were painted with mud resembled a bunch of little boys trying to play cannibal.

One fellow had been out hunting for wildebeest tails which the tribe used for fly swatters. He had with him a rude bow and some poisoned arrows, but no clothing except his ear decorations. The native's chief idea of beauty seemed to be slit ears filled with ornaments.

This strange process begins when a young child has a hole punched in his ears. First a small piece of wood is put into the hole. As he grows older his ears are stretched more and more until the hole is sometimes several inches in diameter.

Another style of beauty among the natives is to glue hair on one another's head. This starts when a member of the family dies. His hair is cut off and is glued into the hair of his relatives. When they die their hair is passed along. Some proud natives boast that they have hair from all their ancestors for a century or so back!

Now the women of the tribe began to file out of the manyetta. There were twenty or thirty of them, all of whom wanted to shake our hands. Although they were very dirty the natives were interesting and made good pictures. But we soon got enough of these ugly smelly people and were glad to move on.

Next day we stayed in camp to make pictures of our own natives who were much more fun. Mr. Johnson got all the boys together and took a picture of the entire camp staff. Ponda-Ponda had his Sunday hat on (there wasn't any top on it). O'sani wore his red shirt which he saves for such special occasions. One of the drivers had on his double terrai which was so big that it looked like a pirate hat. Bucari had his turban wrapped around his head. Pishi wore his apron on which a coffee advertisement was written.

Then we made some movies of our making a Boy Scout of Moko. We showed him the salute, the hand shake, and a good scout grin. The last came natural to him. After him we made scouts of Mr. and Mrs. Johnson. Finally we tried to get some movies of Kima, the monkey which Mr. Johnson had brought down to camp from Nairobi. But every time we got Kima in a good position, one of the black boys would pass and she would go for him. Kima was tame enough around white people; but if a black came near her she would scream with rage and try to get at him. During our time in camp she bit several of the boys.

Nearly the whole bunch of our boys in camp had been with the Johnsons since they first came to Africa, nine years ago.

There was Bucari, a Nubian, who was our gun bearer. The Nubian tribe has a very high code of loyalty. One rule of the tribe is that a gun bearer can't desert his master. If a Nubian's bwana, or master, is killed by wild beasts or by savages the gun bearer is disgraced and he is not allowed to return to his tribe. In most cases he commits suicide.

Bucari was one of the strongest men we had ever seen. His muscles were tremendous. He could lift as much as we three put together. Mr. and Mrs. Johnson called Bucari a perfect African gentleman, to which we all agreed. He was the headman of the safari and he chingered all the meat for the other boys.

If we had one of the strongest men in camp,

The Main Camp in Tanganyika.

"WE WERE NOT EXCITED. OH, NO! WHAT DID FOUR LIONS MEAN TO US, PARTICULARLY WHEN THEY WERE

we also had the raggedest. Ponda-Ponda, a porter, wore clothes that must have been worn by Noah. He had a coat that hung on him only by two or three slender threads. Why it never fell off was a mystery. He wore a hat that looked fairly good from the side; but there was no top to it. His pants were nothing but patches that were falling apart.

Ponda-Ponda was always hinting for us to give him clothes. He used to say to us, "When you go home, I stand at station and say, 'Good-bye, Dick, Good-bye, Dave, Good-bye, Doug.' I have new clothes then. I got old clothes now, but I have new clothes then. Where I get new clothes? Dick, Dave, Doug know where I get new clothes! Ha—Ha—Ha!"

Ponda-Ponda had no special job. His main purpose in life seemed to be to talk all the time. He skinned better than the skinner did and was a better porter than the other porters. But he did as little of either as he could. His favorite pastime was fishing. When Mrs. Johnson ran out of fish hooks she just had to ask Ponda for some. He always had them. On safari he carried with him a little bag full of his personal belongings. In this he had lucky trinkets, tobacco, fish hooks, and everything else he had

collected. He smoked tobacco which came in
big round balls, into which he put sugar to
sweeten the taste. The odor of the mixture
was terrible.

O'sani, the sixty year old kitchen "toto,"
was an interesting character. He was more like
an American negro than any of the others in
camp. We never saw him when he wasn't laughing. He would joke and play with us at any
time. The other boys made fun of him and
called him a toto (child). O'sani would answer
them and say, "Sure I play with the totos. Who
do I get my money from, you or bwana?"

He had learned somewhere to say "yas," and
"honey-boy." This was about all the English
he knew. He used to sit by the fire and say,
more to himself than anyone else, "Honey-boy!
Come here, honey-boy. Yas, yas, yas, honey-
boy."

One night we had cocoanut pie for dinner.
When O'sani brought the pie in Mr. Johnson
asked, "I wonder who made that pie? It looks
mighty good."

As Mrs. Johnson knew that he would make
some such remark, for he was always making
jokes about her pies, she had instructed O'sani
to say, "I made the pie this morning."

O'sani thought that he'd add a little more to show off his knowledge of English. He waited until Mr. Johnson repeated the question. Then he answered in a grave voice:

"Honey-boy, I made thisee pie thisee morning. Yas, honey-boy, pie, pie, honey-boy."

Just then, it dawned upon him that he had called his bwana, "honey-boy." For a second he was horrified. Then, when he saw Mr. Johnson laughing, he laughed too and ran back to the kitchen.

After dressing in the morning we usually went to the cook shack where O'sani would be making coffee.

"Hello, toto," we'd say.

"I'm no toto," he'd laugh. "I'm old. Poor O'sani is old and losing his hair." At this he would take off his hat and show us that he was getting bald. But by the time breakfast was ready he had finished pitying himself and was satisfied with the world in general.

He had a dance that we liked to make him do. He would shimmy up and down, humming and singing a little song of his own origin. At such times he was more like a monkey on a stick than a human being.

Suka, a Meru about fifty years old, was also

55

a "boy." He was the boss of camp. Sometimes when he thought that we were not eating enough, he would fill our plates full of food and stand beside us until we ate it. He even bossed Mr. and Mrs. Johnson around.

Once Mrs. Johnson told Suka that she wanted a bath at four o'clock. Suka filled the tub and got everything ready only to find that Mrs. Johnson was preparing to go out after pictures.

He went up to Mr. Johnson and said, "Memsab wanted a bath. Now she must take it. Don't let she go out without her bath." He then folded his arms and stood in front of the tent, looking like a black Napoleon. Mrs. Johnson laughed, but she took her bath.

Dave called Suka, Mussolini. Every morning at about four-thirty he came into our tents with a "good morning." At first we answered "good morning," then went back to sleep, but later we knew that it also meant get up.

One morning Suka went over to wake Dave. He did so, but Dave didn't get up. Suka said, "Are you sick?"

Dave answered, "No."

Then Suka said, "Well, you get up then." When Dave remained in bed, Suka shook the cot and threw him out. Then he said, "Next time, you get up."

After Suka had gotten us up in the morning, along came Mogo, the boy from the Congo, with a basin of water.

"Hello, Mogo," we called to him.

Then came the stern reply, "*Apana, Jua, Hallo.*" In other words "I don't understand hello." Seemingly, he didn't wish to kid with the totos. He often got those spells wherein he didn't want to play with us but we always brought him to rights by tickling him until he called for Suka. Suka would arrive on the scene and tell us not to play or talk with Mogo because it kept him from working.

The next time we'd see Mogo after such incidents he'd tell us not to talk to him for then he couldn't work. Then he'd edge up to us and whisper, "*Suka Grai,*" meaning Suka was crazy. This amused him, for he'd run away laughing with two big dimples showing on his cheeks. If we asked Mogo how he got his dimples he would say, "I cut them out with a big knife," or "*Sharri mango.*" (Meaning the business of God.)

The Johnsons got Mogo out of jail when they were in the Congo. Although only fifteen years old the boy had two wives at the same time. That would have been all right but he did not support them; thus the jail sentence.

In addition to the regular boys there were four or five Waccoma natives who usually worked around camp. They carried water and wood and looked after the still. There was one of them who seemed to be fond of music. Every day he made some new kind of instrument. Sometimes he would take a bunch of tin cans, fill them full of pebbles and tie them around his ankles. When he danced, the rattle of the pebbles made an awful racket, which seemed to please him very much.

One day when we were just about in the middle of the thorn section we had a puncture. As we were changing the tire, we noticed among the boys a Waccoma native whom Mr. Johnson had not told to come along. Mr. Johnson asked Bucari, the headman, about it. Bucari replied that the Waccoma was a rain doctor whom he had brought in case it threatened to rain. He pointed out that the doctor had his rain stick, a bunch of long grass in which were bound a feather, some fruit of the wild egg plant, and three or four little black balls from the thorn trees. When he wished to drive away the rain, said Bucari, he waved his stick back and forth chanting all the time in the Waccoma language. We noticed afterwards that the rest of the boys would always laugh at him while he was performing, but they probably laughed just because the white people did. The boys thoroughly believed in his power and brought him along whenever we took a trip.

Just as we reached camp the next day it began to rain a little. At once the rain doctor jumped from the truck and began to chant, waving his magic stick. The other boys looked at us, saw we were laughing, then broke out laughing themselves. However, in a few minutes, the rain cloud passed over and the rain stopped. Whereupon the "doctor" came over to us with a satisfied smile on his face. With grave faces we thanked him and told him that he had done his work well. So he was perfectly satisfied. A little later we heard the boys discussing it. They were just as strong as the doctor in their belief, in spite of their laughing.

One day we got back to camp when it was raining so hard the rain doctor couldn't make it stop. As we hadn't had a swim since we left home we thought the next best thing would be to put on our swimming suits and have some fun.

We did so and in running around over the ground, which had recently been burned, we got as dirty and black as the natives.

The boys saw us playing around and had a great laugh. They said we were all "*toto grai*," (crazy boys). They could not understand our wanting to stay out in the rain.

We decided we'd have some fun with the boys. So we went over to the cook's fire where all the boys were sitting. As our first victim, we picked O'sani, the best natured one of the bunch. We walked up to him and began to do a few exercises, such as touching our toes without bending our knees, and sinking down on one knee without losing balance. O'sani, with his face all agrin, began to try to do as we did. But as he was an old fellow every time he'd try the first, his knees would bend; and every time he attempted the second, he fell over.

Just then Mr. Johnson, who had been watching the proceedings, called us over for some pictures. He made some dandy film of O'sani. Then Mogo, shy and bashful, came over. We got him to play leap frog, and his form was great. We laughed at Mogo, but when O'sani tried to stand on his head, we nearly had a fit.

DOUG GIVES MR. JOHNSON LESSONS IN OPERATING A
MOTION PICTURE CAMERA.

Four Masai Ladies Interview the Scouts.

It was fine for the movies and Mr. Johnson got it all.

After dinner that night Mr. Johnson told us the names which the boys had given us. The boys of a safari, even though they know the names of the various people, always give them some names of their own. So after a few days, we received our names.

Dave, who was always talking and joking with the boys, they called "*Bwana Menano,*" meaning "master talk all the time."

Doug, who eats very slowly and talks the same, was given the name of "*Bwana Poli-poli,*" meaning "master who is very slow."

One night when Dick was down with them, they saw him cleaning the mud and dirt from his fingernails. Some time later, they saw him combing his hair. From this he got the name of "*Bwana Mardadi,*" which means "master pretty."

We gave Dick a great razzing about this.

# CHAPTER VIII

### DICK AND DAVE GET LIONS

SO far only Doug had got his lion. Now it was up to the other two of us to get ours. Of course we went out practically every day. But we had several adventures before either fellow got his shot.

After breakfast one morning Bucari came into camp with the report that there were fourteen lions on zebras near camp. This seemed promising, so we all set out after lion pictures. We'd only gone about a half mile from camp when we saw nine lions. As during the night before we had heard lions roaring near camp, these nine were perhaps the same ones. When we first saw them they were in a donga getting a drink of water. Three of them were sleeping on an ant hill and gave us a chance for some good pictures. The others ran away as soon as they saw us coming.

We had left these three lions and had gone

another half mile when we saw three more, trotting along through very high grass. The grass was so high that we could barely see their heads. As they were on the opposite side of the donga from us we couldn't get any successful pictures.

Later we saw two very large lions in amongst some palm trees. One of them had a golden mane, the other a shorter mane and not so pretty. The two of them were trotting towards the thicker bush and palm trees near a donga. When they saw us they stopped and growled. We didn't go any closer to them for we thought they might charge.

Keeping near a little valley in search of what pictures we could get, we suddenly came upon two shaggy beasts peering at us from the depths of the valley. At first they looked like buffalo because of their huge proportions. When we came to an open space there opposite us, not a hundred yards away, were two of the largest lions in Africa. Their manes were plainly a foot long, perhaps more. This was an unusual thing for African lions, for the thorns and bushes usually tear the manes off.

Even Mr. and Mrs. Johnson who have been in Africa for nine years and have seen perhaps as many lions as anyone had never witnessed such a sight. When Mrs. Johnson saw them, she just gasped.

Just then, one of the lions walked forward a few feet. As he moved, his mane shook and swayed from side to side. Then Mr. Johnson rubbed his eyes and whispered, "I'd rather have a picture of those lions than anything else in Africa!" To do this would be a difficult job for the lions were plainly old and timid. But a single picture would be worth as much as any other trophy in Africa.

Mr. Johnson decided right then and there to try to get a photograph even though it took several days' work.

We started by getting a zebra kill and sprinkling it with catnip. We dragged it up near the lions. Then we withdrew about two hundred yards and watched. It was absolutely necessary to be quiet. There we were, watching hopefully while the lions simply slept. But at the end of the first hour, they got up and slowly walked away. We certainly were disappointed.

We waited another hour in perfect silence, hoping that they would return, but they must have been aware of our presence and stayed away.

DICK'S IDEA OF WHAT THE WELL-DRESSED LION-HUNTER SHOULD WEAR.

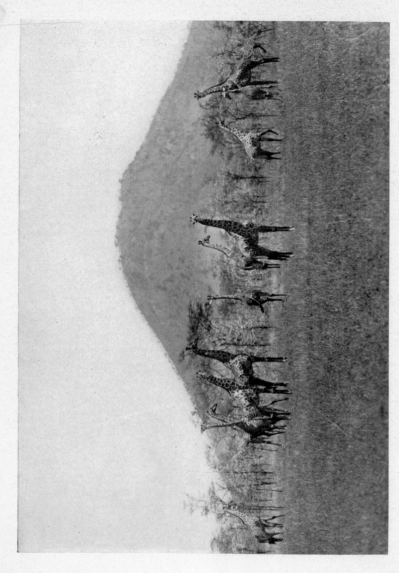

The Giraffes Were the Most Curious of All the Animals.

At the end of the second hour, we were hungry and tired, so we returned to camp.

When Dick learned that he was going to make the trip to Africa he wanted to take his bow and a bunch of arrows which he had used a lot at home. He consulted Mr. Putnam who said that he thought it would be all right. So his scoutmaster made him a new bow and he ordered some new arrows.

On arriving in Nairobi, Dick asked Mr. Johnson about the possibility of his getting a trophy with it and found he approved the idea.

On the morning after seeing the big maned lions we decided to try to get close enough for Dick to get a shot with his bow and for Mr. Johnson to photograph it.

We followed one of the dongas where we usually saw lions and soon saw three. They were on a sand bank on the other side. We advanced as far as possible without frightening them; then Dick took a shot. The first arrow went low, several feet in front of the lion. Two of the animals jumped over into the ground a few inches from the lion's tail. He gave a roar and bounded fifteen feet into the grass.

Dick had failed in his shooting, but Mr. Johnson had made some good action photographs of the whole thing. He had been turning the crank of his camera all the time.

We left these lions and went on looking for more. We soon caught sight of two, but they disappeared before we could get close to them.

This morning the baboons seemed to be out in full force. At our appearance, they scuttled off into the dense bush of the donga and said very uncomplimentary things about us. When it comes to being profane, any baboon could be pitted against a dozen parrots and sailors put together. It was amusing to see them jump from branch to branch, yelling with all their might at us. Another funny sight was seeing a loving parent running along with a small toto clinging to her back.

On our way, Mrs. Johnson spied a lion. We looked through the glasses and made out five others. The six had a kill and were eating on it. We were on the opposite side of the bank. Mr. Johnson took a few pictures, but we were too far away for good results.

We went back to camp so that Mr. Johnson could get some more film and fix his cameras to get some slow-motion pictures.

This time we filled a little rubber balloon with red pepper. Mr. Johnson had put pepper on a kill before and had some fine pictures of a lion sneezing. This time though, he wanted to put a balloon filled with pepper and blown up, inside the stomach of a kill. Then we would make movies as the lion burst the balloon and the pepper flew into his face.

We went back to the spot where we had seen the lions. Only one was on the kill, an old lioness. The others were just a few yards away. Mr. Johnson wanted to scare the lioness from the kill temporarily in order to put in the balloon. But he knew that if we walked up to the kill the lions would all leave. So at last he told Dick to shoot an arrow to frighten her off the kill. Dick tied a handkerchief around his arrow and shot. The arrow thudded to the ground beside the lioness. She gave a roar and ran off a few feet.

If we went up to the kill all the lions would immediately run away. So finally we gave up the balloon idea. Mr. Johnson decided that he would wait for them to come back to the kill and start eating. Then he could get all the pictures he wanted.

But none of the lions seemed hungry. Presently we saw vultures coming for the meat. This, we knew, would bring the lions. As the scavengers swarmed over the kill, one of the big lions came for them. It was interesting to watch him. He was afraid of the strange animals near him (ourselves), but in spite of his fear he refused to let the vultures finish his meal. So when they flocked to the kill and started devouring it he looked at us, hesitated, then finally went for the vultures in great bounds. As soon as he got close to them, the birds flew off a few yards. Having frightened the robbers from his food the lion looked at us, growled, and ran back to the others.

All this made good pictures. Mr. Johnson had a slow motion attachment on his camera, and was having a great time with it.

In time the lions began to seem so harmless that we grew careless. In one case, however, we found we were sadly mistaken about a lion's humor.

We saw a lioness resting near a bunch of reeds. We went closer to get a photograph. She was gentle enough until we got within fifty feet of her. Then she jumped to her feet and stood facing us, the picture of anger. Her black-tipped tail lashed from side to side. She growled and snarled. She opened her mouth until we could see a foot down her throat.

# DICK AND DAVE GET LIONS

We went a few feet nearer and she crouched to spring. Another foot we advanced with our guns in one hand and our camera in the other. Now the lioness crept a few inches in our direction, then, changing her mind, she snarled and sprang back into the clump of reeds. I don't know whether she lost her nerve or whether she was not charging but just trying to scare us. If she was doing the latter, she certainly succeeded. Mrs. Johnson said that the lioness probably had cubs in the reeds. If she did, we're sure that nothing will get them as long as they stay near their mother.

A little farther on we discovered four big lions. One of them was a beauty. His mane was much longer than the average lion's, and his taffy-colored skin in perfect condition. We watched them from about fifty yards, and then got closer, little by little until only a few feet separated us from the animals. We tried to get some snaps of them. But everything went wrong.

Disturbed by our movements, the lions now moved off a way. The truth was that we were excited and our attempts at photographing were just a series of bungles. In fact the lions seemed amused by our silly doings. Finally, one by one, they moved off. The big one who seemed particularly interested in our movements, walked to the edge of the donga where he seemed to fall in. We were waiting for him to appear when Mr. Johnson said, "Oh, well. He's dead by now."

"What do you mean?" we asked.

"What do you think I mean," he retorted. "Why the old fellow probably rolled into the donga and laughed himself to death!"

We saw a funny sight one day when we came upon two large males resting under a tree. As we approached them hundreds of monkeys in the nearby trees broke into a wild chatter. We forgot the lions for a second and watched the little fellows playing among the branches.

One member of the family was seated quietly on a limb, looking very serious when a playmate hit him on his head. A chase started. When they came to grips the offender paid for his playfulness.

One tiny monkey on the same tree under which the lions lay, crawled down the trunk, apparently not knowing the big beasts were there. When he saw them he gave one startled look and scrambled up again. "I'm surely not going to play with those fellows," he yelled to the world.

TEACHING MOGO HOW TO BE A GOOD BOY SCOUT.

MRS. JOHNSON'S CADDY

Meanwhile, Simba caught sight of us and let out a deep roar which was as much as to say that our presence was not wanted. However, since by this time we got quite a kick out of defying lions, instead of going away we went nearer.

We got some fine pictures of these two males, but they insisted on lying down. Mr. Johnson whispered to Mrs. Johnson to make a noise like a cat. This will always attract a lion's attention. She began to meow exactly like an old stray cat wandering around the back yard hunting for food. It sounded so funny that Mr. Johnson got to laughing so hard that he couldn't make pictures. We had a lot of trouble in keeping from laughing out loud.

Then Mrs. Johnson imitated a hyena. It was such a perfect imitation that even the lions were puzzled. They didn't know what to think of a two-legged hyena! One of them, the longest-maned one of the two, ran off from the kill; but we got two good snapshots before he made up his mind to leave.

We followed the maned lion, who was a beauty. Dick got his bow and a couple of arrows ready while we advanced within twenty yards of him. When the lion showed signs of a charge by roaring and lashing his tail, we stopped.

Just then, Mr. Johnson, who was at his movie camera, told Dick to shoot. Dick drew back his arrow and loosed it. When the shaft hit the lion in the back haunch he gave a loud roar and bounded into a donga, none the worse for the experience.

We had just started to follow when we saw a big male lion come trotting along the side of a little ravine and disappear where the other had gone. The lion had horns! We gasped and looked again. Yes. There were two black horns growing out from behind his ears. This lion was certainly one of the rarest species in Africa.

Then we realized what it was. We laughed at ourselves for even beginning to believe a lion could have horns. The maneless lion which we had left on his kill, had seen the other which we had shot go into the donga. He had picked up the head of the kill which was a topi, to take it down to where he could enjoy it with the other. He was holding the head in his mouth in such a way that the black horns stuck up behind his ears! Mr. Johnson was almost sick because he had not been able to get any movies of our "horned lion." But anyway, we had a sight that is granted to very few people.

July 20th was our big day in regards to lions. We got up with the sun and had breakfast. Of course this was not an unusual thing to do, but breakfast was always one of the most interesting features of the trip.

The territory that we were to take in that day was the same as where Doug had shot his lion. We had been out hardly five minutes when we saw four lions under a tree asleep. It was rather early for them to be resting, for they are usually either hunting or eating at six o'clock. These must have eaten all night.

We got up almost close enough to touch them before they awoke. That is the way it seemed; but no doubt they were really wide awake almost as soon as we saw them. They were very tame, and we got within thirty or forty feet of them. One old lioness rose up on her haunches and blinked at us. Then she yawned, showing her great teeth and red throat. After showing us how we bored her, she lay down beside one of the males and began to lick him. The one to whom she was proving her affection seemed not to appreciate her; he rolled over on his other side to get away from her.

We made a number of photographs of this "lion love scene." After a while, they all apparently went to sleep once more so we left them.

Cutting across a short stretch of veldt, we found ourselves in the exact spot where Doug had shot his lion. Just then, Mr. Johnson said, "Stop awhile. Something tells me that if we wait a minute, we will get another for Dave or Dick."

Mr. Johnson's hunch came true; for the minute we stopped we saw out on the plain three fine lions. They had finished eating and were on their way to the donga. As we were a good distance from them Mrs. Johnson took the field glasses to examine them. She said that the first and last ones were very good. They were not as large as the middle one but they had much better and finer manes.

As they seemed to be excellent lions Dick and Dave both decided to try for one. While we had been seeing many lions, we had been waiting for exceptionally good specimens. We started after them at once, but when they saw us, they ran over into a donga before we could get within range and disappeared into the tall grass.

We at once got ready to go up to the donga to

take a shot. Dave chose the .303 Springfield while Dick took a .405 Winchester. Of course, Bucari with his big .470 and Mr. Johnson with another .405 were ready also in case of a charge. When everything was ready we moved slowly forward to the edge of the donga.

Just then the lions ran up the opposite side of the ravine. Dave, picking the one on the left, instantly fired. Close upon the report of his Springfield came that of the .405. Dick had shot at the lion who had run over toward the right.

Dave's lion was hit in the back legs and could not move. He sank down in the grass and lay still. Then we saw the one Dick had hit running away. He had been hit in the leg also, but the shot had not put him down. We decided to go after this latter one to finish him off because it looked as if he might escape. In order not to let him get away wounded, Mr. Johnson and Dick both fired. He went down, one bullet in his heart and one through the lungs, dead.

Now we turned our attention to the first lion, who was beginning to try to get away. When we approached him he gave a short roar and opened his great mouth. Then he sunk down as if he were going to charge. It was a nervous minute. We thought he could not move, yet he now appeared to be ready to charge. Mr. Johnson got ready to shoot if necessary. But Dave was ready now and put two shots into the lion which at once rolled over dead.

When we put the two lions together, we could hardly tell them apart. Dick's lion was just a little larger, but Dave's had a longer mane. We hurried back to camp as soon as possible so the skins would not spoil before the skinner could get to them. On arrival we compared our new trophies with the one Doug had shot several days before. The three lions could hardly have been more alike if they had been triplets!

Mrs. Johnson baked two pies that night in honor of the lion hunters.

JACKALS AT A KILL—DIFFICULT FOR NIGHT PHOTOGRAPHY AS THEY ARE IN CONSTANT MOTION.

GETTING THE CAMERAS SET UP FOR FLASHLIGHT WORK.

# CHAPTER IX

## MIDNIGHT THRILLS

WE all came home agreed about the most exciting adventure of our trip: it was the night we spent in the truck surrounded by hungry lions.

It began one day after lunch when Mrs. Johnson put some food up in a box while Mr. Johnson gave orders for setting up his flashlight apparatus. We didn't know what it was all about until they explained that they were going to set a kill and watch it in order to take a night lion picture.

Luckily for us Mr. and Mrs. Johnson met with no success with the attempted flashlights. No lions came up to their kill all night. And though they heard the two large lions that we had seen the day before very close to the kill, neither animal came up to the cameras.

Mr. Johnson explained that when he had arrived at the kill at dark some Masai natives were there. The Masai had seen the wildebeeste which was being used for bait, and had come over to cut off its tail, which they use for a great many purposes. Mr. Johnson thought the Masai had frightened the lions away. He said that if there were ever any natives which he would have liked to have shot, it was these. They had spoiled the chance of a lifetime!

As soon as the Johnsons had eaten their breakfast, we went out again in search of those special big lions that we had previously located. We spent all morning in the search, going over many miles of plains and following several dongas. There were hundreds of wildebeeste, zebra, and tommies, but not a lion.

We returned to camp at noon all worn out and found some visitors. The Milwaukee Museum party for collecting specimen of African animals, birds, and other natural history subjects was camped about a mile from our camp. They had with them a white hunter, Mr. Pat Ayres, one of the best hunters in Africa. With the party was also Mr. Wells who was going to climb Mt. Kenya. They had all come over to visit us and to discuss the prospects of getting specimens.

After awhile, Mr. Ayres mentioned the fact

that they had come across one of the biggest lions that he had ever seen. They were going back the next day to shoot it.

The minute we heard that, we were all ears. We thought they had seen our two big lions. We began in a nonchalant way to pump them for information. Pretty soon Mr. Ayres caught on and he shut up like a clam. But from one of the others we learned enough to tell us the lions were not our big ones.

The reader may think it was unsportsmanlike not to tell them about the lions. But we knew they would only shoot them for their museum, while we wanted them for pictures.

We had cocoanut pie for dinner that night. It was Dick's birthday, and Mrs. Johnson baked two pies in honor of the occasion. Dick did not get the usual beating that comes with a birthday. When Dave and Doug asked Bucari to help them give Dick sixteen licks the old hunter was shocked. No, sir! He wasn't going to help them beat a white boy! He didn't have anything against him. What had Dick done to them? When they explained to him that it was just in fun, he was tickled to death to help them. The beating was to be at dinner time. However, when dinner time came Dave and

Doug were too busy eating cocoanut pie to bother about it.

For lunch next day we had some ice cream. Mrs. Johnson had made it, and it sure was good. She had a little machine that froze ice or ice cream, and it took only a few minutes to have a big dish of ice cream sitting before us.

As Mr. Johnson decided to use the flashlights again that night he went out at two-thirty to place the kills and to set the cameras. The rest of us stayed in camp.

The method of making flashlight pictures which Mr. Johnson used was quite different from that used by the photographers at home. Instead of opening the shutter and then setting off the flash, the flash and the shutter worked together. When the operator pressed a button, the lamps were set off. As the flash began, a cap shot up to the top of the lamp striking a spring; then it flew down again and pressed the shutter lever of the camera just when the flare was at its brightest. In this way the camera could be set at one three-hundredth of a second. In using a slower action, the animal subject, if he jumped when the flare goes off, might blur the picture. With the Johnson method no movement showed in the photograph.

A Lion Family at Home.

"Bwana Mardadi" Shows Them Up.

About sunset we arrived on the spot where the kills had been set and arranged the cars so that the backs of them would be facing the kill. Mr. and Mrs. Johnson stayed at the edge of a donga with the plains behind them. We were between two dongas and within shouting distance of the Johnsons. The back of our truck faced the dead zebra with the cameras in between.

The sides of our truck were of heavy wire. As it had a good top, only the front and back had to be closed. These were made secure by lashing poles across both openings. After we got into the body of the truck the boys wired poles across the front. This partition shut off the front seat from the rest of the truck.

We knew that we were safe from lions; yet we all felt a little nervous when Mr. Johnson left us. We changed to our pajamas while it was still light and ate the lunch which Mrs. Johnson had prepared for us.

Just as we started to eat Dave said something about this being our last meal on earth. We all laughed; but little remarks like that at such a time make one feel rather ill at ease. To be sure, we had arranged with Mr. Johnson to fire the rifle twice if we needed him, but what good would that do if he were a considerable distance away and the lions only a few feet?

After eating lunch in a silence broken only by a few strained whispers, we crawled under the blankets. We had been told that if the lions heard a human voice they would instantly run. It was likely, though, that even if the animals were not afraid, we would have whispered because we were all so excited. Doug said something about getting a lion into the truck and then jumping out. This started Dave laughing. He buried his head in the pillow and almost had hysterics. We finally thought he was crying, but he called out, "You fellows are going to kill me yet!" Then we all started laughing and trying not to make a sound at the same time.

We had been turned in about half an hour when we suddenly heard a bone crack. We slowly raised up and peeped out between the poles across the opening at the rear. Instead of the hyenas we had expected, we saw an old male lion. He had a short mane but he was a big fellow. When we saw him, we all started shaking. It was not so much the fright as it was seeing a big lion just a few feet away.

As we watched he started eating away on the

zebra. We could hear him very plainly as he tore out great hunks of meat. Now and then he snarled and growled deeply in his throat. We turned the flashlight on him; but instead of running away, he only crouched down behind the dead body. For several minutes we watched him. After a while he got over his fear of the light and began once more to eat. Mr. Johnson says that he thinks the lions believe the flash of a hand light or of a flare to be only lightning in the sky. Whatever this one thought, he showed no fear.

Finally we started whistling to make him hold his head up. When we first whistled, he ran off a few feet but soon returned. We whistled again and he just looked up at us. Now Dick caught hold of the two wires which controlled the flares. To set them off the wires had to be touched together. The lion looked up just then but was not in the right position. Dick was going to whistle once more, but just as he drew in his breath, the flare went off with a loud report and a blinding flash. His hands had been shaking so that the wires had touched without his knowing it.

We kidded Dick about that for the rest of the trip. But from the way the truck was shaking at the time, our hands and bodies were trembling as much as his.

At the flash the lion ran off, blundering through the bushes. He was blinded by the light for some time.

Then this conversation took place. Dick said: "I bet the lion wasn't even in the picture."

Doug answered: "I expect Mr. and Mrs. Johnson think we are crazy, taking a picture at this time of night."

Dave said: "Boy! That was certainly a relief to see that lion run."

In a few minutes we heard Mr. Johnson calling. Doug whispered: "I bet they are laughing at us. They're saying, 'Those boys probably photographed a hyena, mistaking it for a lion.'"

Mr. Johnson called: "What did you get?"

"Only a lion," we answered in a nonchalant way.

"Well, go to sleep," he yelled back. "We'll see in the morning."

We all crawled under our blankets, thinking it was all over for the night. This was about eight o'clock. We remained awake for half an hour, then dropped off to sleep.

Several hours later, we were awakened by a

violent shake of the truck. We heard growling
outside. After some minutes of lying in bed,
shivering with both fright and excitement, we
got up enough courage to shine our lights out
the back. Just under us was an old lioness
calmly chewing on a tire! Twenty-five feet
away on the kill, we saw four other lions. And
as we watched two more joined in. Then the
old lioness went back to the group. There
were three big males with manes, three females,
and one toto, or young one.

Surely we believe it was the most exciting
moment of our lives, and also one of the most
interesting.

In spite of their fierce looks, the lions were
exactly like a bunch of cats, quarreling over a
meal. They lay there, one at the head of the
zebra, two at the back, two at the side, and one
on the haunches. The toto stood off a few feet,
watching his chance to slip into the feast. Our
light seemed not to bother them for they just
looked up now and then and blinked. However, one of the males, the one whom we had
made the picture of before, seemed a bit sus-
picious. When we moved the light, he would
crouch down behind the carcass. Perhaps he
had been frightened by the flash of the camera

flares. But he soon got over his fright, and took his place among the others.

After a while the toto crawled up beside one of the big fellows. As long as he kept to his place he was allowed to eat. But once when he got up too close and started for the same bit of meat as one of the others, the big male rose up and gave him a slap. It seemed a light blow, but it sent the youngster sprawling into the grass. He jumped up and ran over to the other side of the zebra where he lay down beside a lioness, probably his mother.

We almost laughed aloud. The scene might well have been that of a human family at a meal. Certainly it was far different from our conception of the family life of a lion. And yet it was typical. For a lion's whole life is spent in search of food. He kills, eats, and sleeps. We had seen what happens every night or so.

However tame and domesticated we might think them, when we heard the growls and deep guttural rumblings as they gulped down large hunks of meat, we could not think of them other than as lions, rulers of the plains and forests.

After we had watched them for some time by the light of our Eveready flashes we noticed that one of the cameras had been knocked down.

We were just discussing this in whispers when one of the big lions left the kill, walked over to the fallen camera and began chewing on it. Then he grabbed it in his mouth and started dragging it away. Suddenly in some way one of the legs of the tripod flew up and hit him, he jumped almost twenty feet. In a few minutes he came back to it; slowly at first, but when he saw it did not move, he pounced upon it.

We felt that there was nothing we could do. None of us would have got out of the truck for any three hundred dollar camera. In a few minutes one of the lions left the zebra and came over to the other camera which was still standing. She rubbed her head against it and chewed the wires connecting the cameras with the flares. We whistled and hissed to frighten her from it, but it did no good.

Finally Dick yelled, "Scat, you heathens, scat!"

Then Doug shouted, "Get away! We've told you twice!"

The sound of our voices finally frightened the lioness from the camera and scared the others from the kill for a while. They soon returned, however, and continued their meal.

We watched them for about an hour before we

lay down again. But just as we decided to go to sleep, we heard a slight noise up in the front of the truck. Dick grabbed his flashlight and crawled up to the bars that separated the front seat from the body. Shining his light out through the bars we saw the head of a lioness not three feet away! She had one foot on the fender and one on the floor board; and she had stuck her head up on the seat. When she saw the light, she only blinked her eyes and crawled back down.

We said not a word. It was the first time we had ever seen a lion try to drive a truck, and the sight gave us quite a shock. We came back to our blankets and waited several minutes before we felt like turning in again. We all lay perfectly still for a while and at last dropped off to sleep.

In the morning when Mr. Johnson came over and woke us we told him about the night. He laughed for half an hour. The loss of one of his cameras did not seem to worry him. He said that our experience was worth it if the picture of the first lion was good. Of course the plate in the smashed camera was ruined; but the one in the other was all right.

He and Mrs. Johnson had heard the lions

roaring and growling over on our kill. But they had never suspected there were seven.

When we returned to camp, we were all very sleepy. So after breakfast we lay down for awhile. But we were soon up again.

Bucari was very glad to see us safe. He had feared that the lions might have broken into the truck.

Mrs. Johnson, active and energetic as usual, spent the morning out hunting for lions with Bucari. She was not going to shoot but just find them for picture making. In the meantime, Mr. Johnson developed the picture made the night before.

About the middle of the morning he called us over to where he was developing. He let out a whoop and we came running. We found that there was nothing the matter; he just wanted us to see the negative of the picture we had made. We had been afraid that the lion was not in the right position. But when we saw the negative we were satisfied. We had caught the lion broadside, standing over the kill, a good likeness of the King himself.

Soon Mrs. Johnson returned bringing a story of a new donga. She had seen a lot of game but no lions. Meanwhile Mr. and Mrs. Johnson, hearing our tale of these seven lions (and believing it to some certain extent), planned to go out with flashlights again. They decided to take both cars as before, and stay together in the same place we had been last night.

In the afternoon Dave and Dick with Bucari went out to get a kill for the night's work. They soon got a zebra, and the boys took it to the place Mr. Johnson was going to set his cameras. Mr. Johnson himself went out at four o'clock to see that everything was ready and fix his mechanism. But before he went Mrs. Johnson made us a real delicacy: APPLE PIE A LA MODE! We had never thought of such things on Safari, but miracles will happen. Then we went down to the donga for the night.

Mr. Johnson had the cameras all ready. We placed the truck alongside the Willys-Knight, climbed into it and the boys again wired us in.

We ate the lunch which the cook had put up for us and then prepared to watch. The first thing that was attracted to the kill was a small jackal. A jackal is usually the forerunner of a lion. He locates the kill for the lion, then stands off until he is allowed to eat. In the meantime, he is barking and scolding, which attracts the lion's attention.

This was true now. No sooner had the jackal come to the kill than a lion trotted up. He didn't do anything but watch for he was apparently not hungry. Yet he was not going to let the hyenas get his meat.

After a little sleep we looked out again. Around the kill were seven lions, probably the same seven we had seen before. None of them seemed very hungry. They gnawed at the kill, but they did not gulp down the meat in great mouthfuls as they did the night before.

Again the lions followed their tactics of the night previous. One of them, after carefully chewing the wires of the batteries, carried them away into the grass one by one. Another walked up to a camera and rubbed his bloody mouth against it.

All this would have made a great picture but the batteries were gone. There were only two things to do: either to go to sleep and forget the lions, or to get out and find the batteries. Mr. Johnson did the latter. He called to us, asking us to shine our lights all around the cars and the kill. Then with a sawed-off shotgun in his hand, he walked slowly over to the kill. He could find only two of the batteries but he connected those again. While he was working,

Mrs. Johnson stood beside the car with her rifle. It was a ticklish business, all right.

All this time, we could see the lions, not over fifty yards away, watching him. They were angry, too, at being kept from their meat. Then someone made the usual bright remark about "Daniel in the lion's den," and we all burst out laughing, even Mr. Johnson.

Before the batteries had been taken the lions had posed beautifully for us. Now they were stubborn and would not come to the kill together. One of them, a big fellow with a mane just the color of freshly pulled taffy, kept trotting up, but just as Mr. Johnson would get ready to make a picture he'd run off into the grass.

Just before daylight, no longer hoping for a good picture, Mr. Johnson snapped the camera on the lions; but they were in the grass and did did not show up well.

We slept until six o'clock, then got out to look for the missing batteries. We found them several yards from their original position. One had holes in both sides. The lion's teeth had gone in until they had struck the carbon pole. The camera that had been rubbed by the lion had a coating of blood all over its side. One of the lions had tried to scratch his head on it while his mouth was bloody from eating on the zebra. At least we found no tooth marks on it.

# CHAPTER X

## A MILLION HEAD OF GAME!

"YOU boys simply must have a squint at the tremendous migration of big game that's going on this year," Mr. Johnson said to us one day.

He went on to explain that earlier in the summer while he was in our base camp here at Serengetti the surrounding plains had been covered with herds of zebra, wildebeeste and other animals all moving towards the south. He thought we might catch this strange phenomenon if we went down to the Blanketti River country in lower Tanganyika. That was good buffalo country, too, he added.

So while we were doing our lion hunting he sent a native on about fifty miles below us to investigate. The fellow didn't return for a week. When he did return he was very enthusiastic over the country. He said there were

# A MILLION HEAD OF GAME!

"Mingi bogu, mingi faro." That is, "Many buffalo, many rhino." And the game was as plentiful as the leaves on a tree, he declared.

We didn't know just how much of the story to believe. The natives, while they do not mean to lie, sometimes tell all kinds of stories. For instance, if you ask one whether there are lions, he will say, "Yes," knowing that you want to be told yes. But if you put the question the other way and say, "There are no lions here, are there?" he will answer, "No."

We started out for Blanketti early on the morning of July 29th. Mr. Johnson had set the alarm clock for four-thirty. We had a cup of tea and a quick breakfast of hot beans and were off before six.

The trail to Blanketti led through the hills, and as it wound about the slopes of them we could see the land below covered with tiny black dots. They were the thousands of head of game, mostly wildebeeste and zebra, with which the Serengati Plains teemed.

A little later we dropped down to the veldt again. As we drove through it trying to dodge the overhanging branches we saw our first herd of giraffe, eighteen of them grazing among the trees.

There were three or four little totos among the herd. One of these was so small he could hardly walk, his head coming up only to his mother's stomach. Every now and then he would stop and turn to look at us. When he did his mother would also stop to see that nothing happened to her baby.

In the herd was also an old bull who seemed to be very sick. He could hardly walk and came lagging along far behind the rest of the crowd. We followed these giraffe across the veldt for several miles until they joined another herd of nine. Together, they made the largest herd we had seen.

The giraffe is the most awkward animal in Africa. His front legs are much longer than his back ones. When he runs, his back rises up and down like a horse on a merry-go-round. He is also about the most defenseless animal, having no way to protect himself save using his front legs to kick. This is of very little use against a lion or leopard. Indeed, against a lion the giraffe is almost without protection. He can't even run as fast as a lion.

We reached Blanketti River about noon on the second day. Our guide, Shai, informed us that the camp site he had selected was an hour's

READY FOR FLASHLIGHTS.

DICK LOOKS OVER A POISONED ARROW.

ride across the river. So we decided to postpone lunch until reaching the spot. But just as we started again, one of the two trucks hit an ant bear hole and broke the rear axle. There we were, three hundred miles from the nearest garage at Nairobi and unable to move. The only thing to do was to go on over to our new camp and then return in our other car for the load of the broken down truck.

One exceptionally bad donga had to be passed. All the trucks were unloaded and after they had gotten over, the loads were carried across by the porters. For this job, some wandering Wassacoma were used. When their tasks were over, Mr. Johnson gave each of them two shillings. They didn't like this one bit; what they wanted were pennies. It took a lot of explaining to make them understand that shillings were worth much more than pennies.

The camp site picked by Shai proved to be a poor one. It was near water and was under big trees which gave shade; but it was not high enough. The tsetse fly was everywhere.

This pest is perhaps the greatest plague of Africa and makes it almost impossible to raise cattle or horses in certain parts of the African continent. When an animal is bitten by the fly it almost invariably dies of sleeping sickness. Human beings are also susceptible to the disease; but very few ever die and relatively few even get sick, we were told.

The bite of a tsetse is very annoying. It hurts as much as a bee sting and causes a painful swelling. To be in a section of country with the fly is just like going into a swarm of mosquitoes that bite three times as hard as the average. Doug once said, while we were in camp at Blanketti, after slapping a fly, "I wish that six more flies would bite me. Then I will have been bitten by two million even!"

Just before sunset, or rather at about five-thirty, for the sun doesn't set down along the equator until about six, we were all sitting in front of the tents doing nothing when we started talking about hill climbing. Suddenly Dick looked up and said, "How much am I offered to climb up to the top of that hill and wave my handkerchief?"

Mr. Johnson laughed and said, "Five dollars." Dave said he would make it two dollars. They were just joking and thought Dick was too. But when we joshed him, he grabbed his gun and started out up the hill. As Mrs. Johnson had said something about there being buffalo and rhino near the foot of the hill, he thought it best to take a .405.

"The first part of the climb was easy," he told us later. "But when I reached the actual hill, though, it was real work. The steep side was covered with small rocks and loose shale. Just before I reached the top, I glanced up and saw something that looked more like a rhino than a rhino does. I almost turned and ran down the mountain. I had a gun, but what did I know about shooting rhino?

"Walking up a few feet, I nervously threw a stone at him. It hit, but he did not move. I advanced a little further and threw another. Still the rhino did not stir. I finally got up within fifteen feet and threw a large rock. Then I saw my rhino was only an ant hill which was formed exactly in the shape of a large rhino, even having two lumps for the horns. I have never felt more relieved in my life.

"I soon reached the summit of the hill and stood for several minutes, waving my handkerchief. A few hundred yards below the top on the way back, I saw Doug. He told me that he had started just after me. When I saw him, he looked as though he had been running. He said that when he got to the foot of the hill a big jack rabbit had jumped from the grass just in front of him. He had been so startled that he had set out up the hill at a run. When we got back it was dark."

The whole incident shows how jumpy we were at times due to there being so many wild animals about.

We got a great laugh out of Mogo one morning. Dick was in front of the tent taking a few simple exercises. Mogo came in with the water for the basin and stopped to watch.

Dick kept on, without saying a word and pretended not to notice Mogo. Pretty soon he began to bend over and touch his toes without bending his knees. He motioned Mogo to try the trick.

Mogo leaned over as far as he could but did not reach below his knees. As he felt ashamed he gave a mighty lunge to get lower. At this a ligament or muscle or something gave a crack in his back. Whereupon he let out a yell, his face turned white, and he went lickety-split back to the kitchen where the other boys were. He would not come out again until Mrs. Johnson, "memsab," assured him that his back was not broken!

When we got up this morning, we were all

"After a While He Got Over His Fear of the Light and Began Once More to Eat."

ready to see rhino and buffalo. Shai, our guide, had told Mr. and Mrs. Johnson of several places where he was sure we'd see them.

We started out over some of the roughest country we'd ever seen. Shai's route led first through a long stretch of "tinga-tinga," meaning ground that is swamp in the rainy season, but is covered with long grass during the dry season. As a result it is terribly bumpy. Next we went through a lot of thorns. In half an hour we had two punctures. Luckily we had two spares.

We were bumping along when we suddenly saw a bunch of black specks off in the distance. Shai whispered, "Bogu."

When we looked where he was pointing we saw a great herd of buffalo. Their bodies were so big that they resembled elephants. Luckily for us they were up wind and could not catch our scent. By careful maneuvers we went up to within a hundred yards of them. Suddenly one of them, a big bull, caught sight of us, whirled around and charged directly for us!

On he came. We loaded all our guns, with hard-nosed cartridges. Gosh, that fellow could run! He soon reached the open space out of the donga, still coming right for us. The earth seemed to shake with his heavy hoofs, and his body looked bigger and bigger. His horns were lowered ready to rip us wide open the moment he struck.

Mrs. Johnson excitedly yelled at Mr. Johnson, who was driving, to "Turn around forward, Martin, and face backwards!"

These directions made all of us burst out laughing in spite of the peril of the situation. Mr. Johnson quickly whirled the car around and stopped. Luckily for us, the buffalo also stopped. For a minute or two he shook his head, pawed the ground, and then to our surprise turned and trotted back into the tall grass of the donga.

We didn't know whether it was the stopping of the car or our sudden outburst of laughter that caused the bull to abandon his charge.

The buffalo is one of the most dangerous animals in Africa. He and the leopard are the most aggressive of all the big game. The African buffalo is much larger than our American species. The animal that once swarmed the plains of our great west had a large head, but the rest of his body was small in comparison. The African buffalo has an enormous head, and his body is built in proportion. Some of them are said to weigh a good deal over a ton.

He is possessed of remarkable scent, sight, and hearing. These together with his aggressive nature make him very dangerous.

Mrs. Johnson later told us of a narrow escape she once had with a buffalo. She was walking along the side of a donga looking for lions when she came upon a big bull. Though the buffalo was on the other side of the donga he caught her scent and started to charge. Then, for no reason, he hesitated, turned and ran in the other direction.

She then thought he had gone and continued on her way. About half a mile up the donga she came to a big bush. Suddenly from behind this bush the buffalo charged. He had sneaked along the donga and hidden where he knew his intended victim would pass. Although Mrs. Johnson was not hunting buffalo at the time, when the animal charged there was nothing to do but shoot. She and Bucari who was with her, both fired. The big bull, weighing over two thousand pounds, crashed to the ground just in front of them.

Mr. Carl Akeley, the naturalist and sculptor, told a story that shows in a terrible way the vindictive nature of the buffalo. Two men were out hunting buffalo one day when a big bull charged. He knocked one man down, then made off after the other. The first man quickly climbed a tree but left his gun below. When he turned to look for his companion he saw that the man had been killed. The infuriated buffalo stood over him, pawing at his body, while the man in the tree turned away from the horrible sight. For one hour he sat in the tree, listening to the angry snorts of the buffalo and the sound of the beast's pawing the ground. When the bull finally left the place, the man came down from his perch but could find no trace of his friend except the place where the ground had been torn up. The body had literally been trampled into the earth!

While following the buffalo herd we saw far behind the rest, a toto. He was a little fellow, and from the way he ran, looked as if he had just been born. In a few seconds his mother came back to him. She trotted along beside him for awhile, then ran on to join the herd. A little later she looked back and saw that he was way behind, whereupon she came back to him. It was exactly like a human mother looking out for her child.

Once when we got a little too close the mother stopped, raised her head and started to charge.

But when she saw that we had stopped, too, she turned and went on. We were all very much relieved when she changed her mind.

About the middle of the morning, we saw a beautiful roan antelope. As the roan is a very rare animal and makes a wonderful trophy, Doug went after it. When he got within a hundred yards he fired, but the shot went high. Instantly the antelope set off for the hills in a steady gallop. Doug followed at a run. As we watched Doug and the roan disappear in the trees, we began to think that we would have to wait for several hours. But after chasing the antelope for over three-quarters of a mile, Doug gave up the useless pursuit and came back, bearing a look of discomfiture—which made us all laugh.

The rest of the morning was uneventful until just before we reached camp. There, only about a mile from our tents, we saw to our astonishment a herd of sixty or seventy buffalo. In the herd were many large bulls, some looking as big as a house. Through the glasses we could see that they were watching us. Mr. Johnson managed to get a few pictures; but the herd made off before we got very close.

The next few days of our camp at Blanketti

were something of a disappointment. It was true that we had come to find buffalo, and had seen a good many of them. But the other game was scarce and there was no sign of the big migration.

Mr. Johnson concluded that the best thing to do was to move camp back to Serengetti where we had spent the first two weeks. We were sure of finding plenty of game there; and where the game was, lions were certain to be.

About noon we left our Blanketti River camp for Serenerra. We had to abandon the truck with the broken axle. The other, loaded with the back axle of the broken truck, the food, and bedding, was so full that we had to leave the tents until we could return for them.

Then the spectacle for which we had come so far suddenly loomed up before us.

It was one of the most wonderful sights imaginable. We had just come out of the hills covered with thorn trees and were dropping down to the plains. Across the plains were more hills. But in front and behind us stretched the veldt as far as we could see. In front the plain was bare, but behind it was divided by a strange *black line almost a mile wide and several miles long.*

At first this line resembled a long black snake

of mammoth proportions lying at full length across the land. Then as we studied it more closely, we could make out that it was entirely composed of animals! Hovering over the animals were scores of birds.

With the help of the glasses we could distinguish zebra among vast herds of wildebeeste that made up the biggest part of the line. And there were hundreds of Grant's gazelle, tommies, kongoni, and topi on the outskirts of the main body. All these, together with the lions and leopards that were sure to be hiding in the long grass watching for a kill, made up what is called the big migration.

"The sight of your lives!" exclaimed Mr. Johnson, as we stood silently and watched the extraordinary picture.

# CHAPTER XI

## IMPALLA, WART HOG AND TOPI

ON the way back we looped around more to the east to get among some of the rarer animals. Arriving in rolling country we came to a lovely donga, wider than the average and much more thickly vegetated. Doug called the place "Sheltered Valley," a name that stuck.

It was early August now, and the end of our adventures painfully near.

On the 10th we all started the day out right by doing a good turn. It was this way. With Mrs. Johnson, we went out to look for meat. Dick wanted to get an impalla. As usual, Bucari went along to shoo any familiar lions away with his .470.

After a while we saw three cheetah ahead of us in a clump of trees. When they saw us, they started off at a trot. Mrs. Johnson noticed something brown dangling from the mouth of one of them. Upon getting a bit closer, we saw

DINING DE LUXE—WHERE THE COCOANUT PIES WERE SERVED.

A Lion Enjoys Supper.

that it was a small animal. Then we heard a pitiful cry, and we knew that the poor beast was still alive. The cheetah dropped its burden and ran on. We stopped and found the little creature to be a baby impalla which we cared for while Mrs. Johnson and Bucari ran after the cheetah.

Soon I heard the loud report of a gun. Bucari returned, bearing the big cat. Mrs. Johnson had stalked the cheetah up a steep hill. She was about a hundred and twenty-five yards from the animal when she fired, the shot hitting him through the brain. He had not suffered, for a brain shot will kill any animal almost instantly.

We took the toto back to camp, washed its wounds and fed him. The only injury we found on him were the teeth marks of the cheetah on his neck. These were not serious. We thought that after making a few pictures, we could turn him loose with some more of his kind. He wasn't hurt badly. All he needed was a little petting to get him over his fright.

We started back to camp. On our way we saw a very unusual animal. It was an albino zebra. He was a very light brown where the black should be. In the herd were six zebra which seemed to have the albino strain but there was only one that was a real albino.

Mrs. Johnson saw a very nice impalla on the way back. It was Dick's turn to shoot. The impalla was hard to approach as all of them are, so Dick had to shoot from about a hundred yards. The first shot missed, but the second went true. He used the Springfield .303, for it is the best rifle we had for antelope.

The afternoon we spent in a general "go-over" of the country. When there was nothing particular to do, we got a great kick out of just looking at the various animals.

The hyena smelled the little impalla, for they howled around camp all night. Mr. Johnson had a trap set for hyena. It was built of heavy logs with a trap door. This morning we heard a howl coming from the direction of the trap, and upon investigating, we found a small jackal in it. It was taken out and put into a larger box for future reference in regard to pictures.

Mr. Johnson thought that the little impalla needed some exercise, so he got out a rope and tied the little fellow up. In a minute he got loose and was going on a run across the veldt. He surely didn't look sick now. Dick, Dave, and Doug started out to catch him. It was no use, though, because he was running about thirty miles an hour. Then all the boys from camp came after him. The impalla ran until the rope which was dragging from his neck caught in some bushes about a mile from camp. Then it was an easy job for Mogo to catch him. We knew then that there was nothing wrong with the impalla.

Later in the morning we took the little fellow back to where we had caught him. We thought that if we turned him loose near some herd of impalla, he would follow them. In a few minutes we saw some way up on the side of a hill. Going up as near as we could without frightening them, we put the toto in a little cleared space of ground. We petted him for a minute or so and then started away. We looked back after a while. He was following us. We had only kept him one day, yet he was so tame that he started after us instead of going up to the herd of his own kind above him.

We should have liked to keep him for a pet, but we knew the fate of most wild animals that are put into a cage or pen. We knew that the best thing to do was to take him to the impalla herd. We did this, taking him away up on the side of the mountain. Then we ran away.

This time, he didn't follow. He watched us go; then he turned and went bounding up toward the others.

A little later we entered the worst fly district in Tanganyika (in our minds). They nearly drove us crazy. Dave said that he didn't mind them biting him, but when they dug in and tried to make a camp in his flesh they had gone too far.

We had the extremely good luck to see another wonderful waterbuck. Dave wanted one badly, so he took the Springfield, loaded it with soft-nosed cartridges and started after him. You should have seen him stalking. First he went like a real Indian, keeping as close to the ground as possible. When he had got within range, he fired and hit the waterbuck in the flanks. The buck ran off with Dave after him. Every few yards, Dave would jump behind some tiny tree and pretend to hide. The waterbuck looked amused at this. Dave fired twice more. The waterbuck died all right, but we insist to this day that it died of laughter.

On the night of August 20th, it seemed as if all the night animals of Africa had combined in a great demonstration for our benefit.

A bunch of hyenas started the show. There was some of the meat from the impalla which

THE DEAD CHEETAH AND THE RESCUED BABY IMPALLA.

DAVE SHOWS MRS. JOHNSON HOW TO SHOOT.

was hanging from a tree near the fire. The hyenas, always hungry, smelled it and came up towards the fire. The fire kept them away, but all night long they howled and laughed. One of them would give a dismal, howling wail, sounding like a lost child. Then the whole bunch would break into a fit of laughing. It sounded as if all the maniacs and insane of the world had broken loose and were laughing at the efforts of their keepers. Some people think the laughing of the hyenas is funny, but to us it was a horrible sound, their shrieking, wailing laughter.

In addition to the hyenas, the hyrax or rock rabbits, that live up among the rocks just behind camp, kept up their squeaking all through the night.

A herd of wildebeeste just about one hundred yards from our tents sounded exactly like a whole mob of Fords all blowing their horns at once. Some travellers in Africa, new to the country, wake up in the night, wondering if they have camped on a highway because of the honking of the wildebeeste.

In small herds, all around our camp, were zebra. They are stupid and nervous beasts. Every now and then they would stampede at some slight sound.   As they went tearing off in any old direction, they sounded not like horses but like terriers with their sharp, quick barks.

There were two lions over in a donga behind camp and the old fellow in front of camp.   They were either very hungry or quite cheerful, for they roared and grunted every ten minutes. The old lion's roar sounded like the thunder rumbling across the veldt.   The sound frightened the zebra into a stampede nearly every time.

Twice during the night, we heard the deep cough of a leopard up in the rocks behind camp.

Once, there was a short silence among the zebra and wildebeeste.   Then we heard a shrill scream, a grunt, and a moan.   A lion or leopard had broken the neck of a zebra.   We found no trace in the morning, though.   He had probably dragged the zebra up into the bushes around the rocks.

Leaving Mr. Johnson at camp, we took the skinner and Bucari with us and went in search of adventure and fresh meat.

A little while later we saw a wart hog.   He had exceptionally long tusks and was a good size in body.   When he saw us, away he went with his tail sticking straight up in the air.   Unlike our pigs at home, the wart hog has a tail over a foot long. Whenever he runs, it looks like a flag pole sticking up on his back. We got up closer to the pig in a few minutes. Doug selected a little seven millimeter rifle. It is small but it hits hard. This time Doug had his gun ready, and shot, bringing him down. At the noise of discharge hundreds of birds arose, and dozens of unseen animals scuttled away in the grass and bush.

I have seldom seen anything as ugly as that wart hog. There were four big knots sticking out on his face. These give him his name for they look like big warts. On his neck was a short, bristling mane, and there was no hair at all on his face. He was so ugly that he was pretty, even the big tusks that stuck out from his mouth and twisted his lips out of shape.

On his face we found three or four long scars. They had been cut in the past and were healed now. Bucari told us that they were the marks of Simba. A lion had clawed him across the face, and somehow the pig had escaped. This was not unusual, for lions like the meat of a young pig. It was unusual that he had escaped, though.

We followed what we called the Rocky Donga

up into a country where we had never been before. The scenery here was entirely new to us. There were beautiful palm and mimosa trees. Vines and all kinds of creepers hung from the trees. This scenery was just like that shown in the movie, "The Lost World." This was Doug's remark as we were going along beside the donga.

After a while we stopped to let the skinner get busy on the wart hog. Of course the minute we stopped by the river, Mrs. Johnson got out her fishing tackle. She fishes at any place and at any time she can get a chance. We slipped and slid through the brush that covered the bank of the river until we found a little pool of water. Bucari went ahead with his big gun, for there were many buffalo tracks around, and we didn't know but what we might come upon some buffalo down at the water. No such thing happened, though, and we settled down for an hour's fishing.

It was in the middle of the day. The sun burned right down on us, and we couldn't get in the shade. There were tsetse flies everywhere. When we slapped at our arms, the flies bit us on the neck. When we hit at them on our necks, they came back to our arms. The

Mid-day on Safari.

THE LION OFTEN SHOWS EXCELLENT MANNERS. AFTER ONE GOOD LOOK HE IS CAREFUL NOT TO STARE

tsetse fly can bite harder than any mosquito and in our opinion, he is one of the worst things about Africa.

You can be sure that the minute the skinner finished his job, we left the place. We believe that even a fisherman like Mrs. Johnson soon would become disgusted with the luck we had. She seemed to be as willing to go as we were.

We also spent some time watching a bunch of monkeys playing. It was next to impossible to get close enough to them to photograph them, but we did enjoy seeing them. When the monkeys saw us coming, they didn't run up a nearby tree, but they started for a tree that was two hundred yards away. They didn't pause in their running, but every few yards, they would give a bound that threw them high enough to see above the grass. While in the air, they turned their little black faces around to see just how close we were. Then, squeaking, they would drop down into the grass and keep running.

Just before dusk, we came to a water hole where we saw a flock of sand grouse. We got four or five with the shot gun and had them for breakfast the next morning.

We have never tasted any meat as good as that of a sand grouse. It is better than any chicken that ever lived. Mrs. Johnson likes the Franklin partridge better, but we think that sand grouse cannot be equalled.

We went back to camp and went to bed early after one of those delicious suppers that only Mrs. Johnson and "Pishi" know how to make.

After we got home from our night's experience in taking flashlights, we slept most of the morning. Mr. Johnson told Dave and Doug that they could take Bucari and go out and get some meat for camp. He also said that if they wanted to they could get a zebra for a trophy. We went out behind camp to look for a zebra before getting the topi. We had to hunt all over the plains before we found a herd. Dave, using a .405, got one with one shot at about one hundred and fifty yards.

While the skinner was busy, Doug took a golf club and ball which he found in the car, and had some fun hitting the ball around the veldt. There are plenty of ant hills for tees and plenty of ant bear holes to knock the ball into.

We started back toward camp, hoping to get a topi on the way back. As soon as we had reached the place where we had started hunting for zebra, we saw a great herd of them. There were so many that we could not see because of the dust they raised as they raced across the plains.

A topi came trotting across in front of us. We went after it. Doug shot several times, then Dave, then Bucari. We kept on shooting and finally shot him. When we returned, Mr. Johnson said that he thought the whole German army was trying to retake Tanganyika!

We packed up and started to Grumitti. Mr. Johnson took his other truck which he used for a developing car, back with us. The trip to Grumitti was not a very pleasant one. The pig holes were very deep and when we would hit one, it was very bad, especially for Dick and Doug who rode in the back of the car.

We had great sport ducking trees on our ride back to our new camp. The top of the car has a piece out for Mr. Johnson and his camera. When he is driving, some of us ride in the back, standing on the floor with our heads sticking above the top. Dick and Doug were riding here on this trip. For several miles, the road ran through a forest of thorn trees. The branches hung over the road and were covered with long, sharp thorns. Every two or three seconds, it seemed, we would have to duck a branch. Sometimes, there was an ant bear hole exactly under the branch. On such occasions, we ducked, but it did no good. When we hit the hole we would be thrown into the air with our heads jammed up against thorns that are strong enough to puncture tires. Even if we did get stuck now and then, though, we enjoyed the ride.

The trip took two hours. Mr. and Mrs. Johnson decided to camp at the same place the Eastman-Pomeroy party had camped two years before. It was situated within fifty yards of a thick donga. When we first saw the donga we thought it was a little too close for comfort. There were leopard tracks not ten yards from the spot on which our tents were pitched. We went down to look for water, we found buffalo tracks in the river bed just below camp. Then to cap the situation, Mr. Johnson told us to be sure to hang a lantern in front of our tent before we went to bed. He said that there wasn't much danger, but he thought it best to play safe. You can never tell what a leopard will do.

As he told us this, Doug's eyes grew wider and wider. Dave began to feel nervous. Dick said, "Are you sure that a leopard will not go near a lantern?"

Then Doug piped up, "How does he know

what it is for? He might not know that it was hung up to keep him out."

Mr. Johnson laughed and said, "Well, if it will ease your feelings, I'll have a boy sleep in front of your tents. The leopard will eat him first."

Dave wondered if they liked dark meat, but he said nothing. He didn't feel in the mood for wise remarks.

# CHAPTER XII

## ELAND, APE AND LEOPARD

ABOUT eleven o'clock next morning we were sitting down to lunch when we heard a motor car coming. We were surprised for we didn't think there were any others in this section. We took the glasses to try to distinguish the make of car. We were afraid it was some safari coming down to hunt.

It made us a little angry to have our picture-making spoiled by other people shooting all around. Of course, it was just as much their country as ours, but we resented their coming. We were getting all worked up when we saw that in the car were Pat Ayres and Mr. Cudahy of the Museum party. They had just come down for a day's look at Grumitti.

We were so relieved that we had a special lunch in their honor. We told them all about the buffalo we had seen on the Blanketti River. When they heard of our seeing the large herds, they were very enthusiastic and said they were coming down as soon as they finished their work at Serengetti.

After lunch we crossed the big donga to have a look at the plains on the other side. When Mr. and Mrs. Johnson had been here before they had nearly always found buffalo, lions, and great herds of eland. The donga had steep sides of sand which slid down and ruined the road the boys had just made. The forest that spread half a mile beyond the donga had to be cut through for the cars to reach the veldt on the other side.

This short stretch of forest was exactly like our ideas of Africa before we came there. It was very tropical with vines and creepers hung from tree to tree and the bushes all having abundant foliage. It felt cool and damp under the trees. The only thing missing from the scene was a leopard coming stealthily down one of the game trails. Then it would have been a complete picture of the Africa of our imaginations.

Some of Africa is all like this. Along the Congo and Zambezi Rivers and in Uganda are real jungles. But most of the Africa we saw was plains with a few trees and almost bare hills.

The section of Kenya and Tanganyika where we spent most of our time was on a high plateau five thousand feet above sea level and the climate was too cold for tropical vegetation.

Soon Mrs. Johnson spotted a herd of waterbuck, one of which had a fine set of horns. She told Dave that it would make a good trophy. Also we knew that the meat of this animal was a favorite dish of our natives. It would taste especially good today because they had a skimpy breakfast that morning out of the remains of the last topi. As their work was heavy it was necessary to keep them properly fed.

It wasn't Dave, however, but Dick who finally got the buck. The natives were delighted and were all for sitting down to dinner then and there. But we had other things to do.

Dave, Mrs. Johnson, Doug and Bucari now went on and had a time of their own. They went over to Rain Hill, which lay about four miles from camp and had good dongas all around it. When they got to the hill they followed a little donga at the bottom. Suddenly Bucari exclaimed, "Eland!" Sure enough

KIMA AND DAVE—READING FROM LEFT TO RIGHT.

A Native Demonstration.

right ahead were two big cows and one bull.

When we shoot for meat we always try to find an animal with good horns so it will make a good trophy. The bull eland had very good horns, was fine meat and we needed some at camp. Mrs. Johnson gave Dave her Springfield rifle so that he might take a shot at it. He shot and hit the first time. Before the eland dropped he had six shots in him. As the boys in camp were without meat Bucari quickly ran up to the eland, and before it was dead cut its throat so the animal could be eaten.

Mrs. Johnson and Bucari took us fishing to Bernagi in the latter part of the afternoon. Coming to the tsetse-fly infested area we saw a large herd of impalla. They presented a formidable array with the beautiful long-horned males strutting proudly in front of the meek females and young. As one of the males had very long horns with an unusual spread, Dave was allowed to shoot it. He knocked it over with the first round from his Springfield. Bucari, jack of all trades, took care of the skinning while the rest of us went fishing.

The pool of our choice was always full of water. We found near it a slide made by crocodiles, a deep track on the mud on the bank as they crawled up from the water and slid back again.

After a few minutes of fishing, Mrs. Johnson hooked a big catfish. She had him almost out of the water when she felt the line pull and then stick. She yanked with all her strength, but the line would not budge. What had happened was that just as she hooked her fish a big crocodile had swallowed it. As the hook was in the mouth of the fish there was nothing to do but cut the line.

We continued for awhile when suddenly we heard a yell from Dave, who was around a bend by himself. "Bucari," he shouted, "bring your gun, quick."

Bucari jumped to his feet, grabbed his gun and started running over to Dave. We were all excited, not knowing whether Dave had seen a buffalo or a lion. Then we heard Bucari break into a fit of laughter. Dave had caught a little fish about the size of a sardine and had yelled for Bucari to bring his gun and kill the monster. Half an hour passed before the gun-bearer stopped laughing.

We fished for awhile and then started back home. Dave and Doug had got the catch of the day, one a sardine and the other a "giant" fish (unknown species of five inches length). Mrs. Bucari did better, having landed twelve or thirteen perch.

On the way home we saw one herd of kongoni with several totos. The adult kongoni looked to be out of proportion, but the little ones looked even more so. Their large ears appeared to be another set of horns. The curious thing about the kongoni was the fact that his back legs went straight down from the end of his back. This sounds queer, but he looked exactly as though his haunches and his tail had been sliced off.

We shot enough partridge for a stew before we got home. The Franklin partridge is delicious, much more so than chicken. We used our .22 rifle and tried to hit them in the head, but we didn't have much success.

Just before we reached camp we found an ostrich egg in the sand. It was almost as big as a football. Mr. Johnson wanted an egg to use in his pictures. He planned to make some film of a cook who has been ordered to poach an egg and serve it on toast. When the cook opens the egg box, he finds only the ostrich egg. He is puzzled and doesn't know how to go about poaching an egg as large as his head. After a while he gets the egg poached, but he cannot find a piece of toast large enough. He finally gives up in disgust and fries the egg.

Next day we crossed the river but went off in a different direction from the day before. Our guide, Shai, took up toward a bit of low brush off in the distance. We were about a half mile from it when the car began to stick. Shai calmly answered our questions as to where we were by telling us that we were just in a tinga-tinga swamp. He seemed to think that a white man's car could go any place. He felt different when he had to get out and help us push. A few minutes later, we got stuck again. At this Mr. Johnson informed the guide in strong words that we did not want to go into any more swamps.

We had no sooner left the swamp on the edge of the Grumitti donga than we ran into a big herd of eland. The eland is a big, cow-like antelope. I say cow-like, but they are far bigger than any cow. Some of them are almost as big as a buffalo. There were two big bulls in the herd we saw that must have weighed at least a ton. They had straight, heavy horns over two feet long. On the ends of the horns of one of them we could see a bit of ivory. Some

THE JOHNSONS AT HOME ON SAFARI.

OUR FAVORITE LOOK-OUT NEAR CAMP.

bulls have ivory tips and some do not. There is probably no set rule about them. The cow eland had even longer horns than the bull though they were not as large.

The herd stood still for a minute while we made some still pictures with our small camera; then it started away. It was interesting to watch them as they trotted along, the big lumps of fat which hang down beneath their necks swinging from side to side. As we approached them they broke into a gallop. They were graceful in spite of their size. When the herd came to the road which ran across their path every one except the totos jumped all the way across it. Then they slowed down to a trot once more and then disappeared over a little hill.

On our way back to camp we had an adventure with a herd of baboons. Just for fun we followed a family of them as they saw us and ran into a donga bordered by trees. As there were several little ones in the bunch, the totos and two or three old ones ran into a big bush instead of running up a tree. We surrounded the bush while Mr. Johnson came running with the Eyemo, his portable movie camera.

There was now a loud chattering and suddenly a big old fellow came charging out of the bush.

We let him go for he was too big to catch. Another old one came out in a few minutes, which we also let go by. One by one the baboons got by us until there was only one left. We wanted to get him because he was a little fellow. So Doug went into the thicket but he didn't catch the baboon. Instead, the baboon caught him, grabbing Doug's thumb in his teeth. Doug caught him by the nape of the neck and finally the baboon let go. Then we got him out of the bushes, put him into a box and took him back to camp. We thought that surely in a few days he would become tame enough to play with Kima, the monkey which Mr. Johnson had brought from Nairobi.

When we got to camp all the boys came running up as usual. Just about the time they got within ten feet of us the little baboon gave a leap to get away. He ran to the end of his rope we had around his leg and the boys scattered. Kima had taught them to beware of monkeys.

One of the drivers in jumping away from the baboon backed into the tree to which Kima was tied. As Kima was excited by the shouting and yelling of the boys she dived for the driver's shoulders and she caught him. The poor fellow nearly had a fit. He gave a scream and jumped

forward again to tear himself from the little ball
of fury that was biting and clawing at his neck.
When he finally freed himself, he left Kima
swinging in the air by her rope around her
waist. But as he leaped forward the baboon
went for his legs. His next leap was sideways,
ten feet, whereupon the baboon lunged on the
small rope, pulled loose and, dashing almost
between the terrified man's legs, scampered up
a tree out of our reach.

As we thought he would stay there awhile we
went to dinner. But in the middle of our meal
we heard a thud. We rushed out and found
that the baboon had leaped to the ground and
had run into the donga. We went in to look
for him, but we found he had joined another
herd of baboons which was the best thing
after all.

In the afternoon, we went over to the plains
where we had seen the eland. We soon came
upon the herd again. Selecting the biggest of
the bulls, and after getting as close as possible
Doug took a shot with the Springfield. He
seemed to have a particular liking for this gun.
He said that it shot straighter than the others.
But it took several shots to bring down his
game. Mrs. Johnson also took a couple of shots

with her .405, because the fat which surrounds the heart of the eland is so thick that a .303 bullet does not kill instantly.

When we went up to the big fellow, we could hardly believe that he was an eland as his body looked more like that of a big buffalo. He was a very good specimen. The horns had a bit of ivory on the tips, and under the neck was a fair-sized beard. The boys cut off a lot of the meat which was very good, tasting much like the meat of a cow. The steak from the rump was particularly delicious. They also saved the head, which Doug wanted for a trophy.

This seemed to be a day for seeing totos. On the way back, we saw toto giraffe, toto impalla, young zebra colts, and little Tommies that were not much larger than my fist.

We also saw a baby hyena. It was just after dark and we were driving along with our lights on. Suddenly a full-grown hyena ran across the road. Then something else came across, squalling at the top of its voice. At first it looked like a tiny black bear cub. Yet we knew that it couldn't be a bear for there were no bears in Tanganyika except the ant bear. It followed the hyena and soon we saw that it was a tiny baby hyena. We chased it around for awhile

"In the Thick of It."

MR. JOHNSON'S OUTFIT ON SAFARI.

until it ran into a hole. A few yards away we saw the mother who had not deserted it at all.

We caught sight of a dik-dik, a very rare animal that is much smaller than even the Tommies. He jumped up from anywhere and vanished suddenly into nowhere.

That night just before we went to bed, Mrs. Johnson told us of an experience of a white hunter who fought and killed a leopard with his bare hands. The story was so awful that it left us pretty nervous for we were within a few yards of a donga where there were many leopards.

Mr. Phil Percival, one of the best white hunters of East Africa, once described a leopard's charge in which the beast had been wounded and yet came for a party of hunters. They all fired, breaking three of its legs. Then one of the men fired a shotgun in the leopard's face. Still the beast kept coming, but finally dropped a few feet from the man. When they examined the body they found its head a mass of crushed bone. The shotgun had blown the skull to pieces; yet the vitality of the leopard kept him running even after his brains had blown out!

The leopard does not, like the lion, hunt together with several others. He lives alone and gets his food alone. It is rather unusual to see a leopard on a kill in the daytime, and we were surprised when once we interrupted one as he was stalking a bunch of Tommies almost at mid-day.

A settler in East Africa is said to have had his dog taken off his own bed by a leopard. When he heard a choking sound in the next room he got up to find out what the disturbance was. Just as he entered the room he saw a leopard jump out of the window. The beast had come into his room and taken the dog off his bed. The choking sound had been the strangling of the dog. When the man got up to investigate, the leopard heard him and jumped out of the window, leaving the dog, very nearly dead.

Bucari had insisted last night that he be allowed to sleep in front of our tent with his .470 by his side. He told Mr. Johnson that it would not be safe for us to be in the tents by ourselves without protection. After hearing of so many lions and leopards, we were glad to have him on guard.

# CHAPTER XIII

## END OF THE TRAIL

JUST before we had to go home O'sani announced that he'd decided to go with us to America. He said he would be our boy if we would give him no work to do but to shine shoes. He liked to shine shoes.

However, Mrs. Johnson changed O'sani's plans. She told him that if he went to America he would have to wear a tie. This was a blow; but after O'sani thought it over he decided that he could do that. Then Mrs. Johnson added that he'd also have to eat with a knife and fork. This was the last straw. Knives and forks were dangerous, he said. Not even the wonders of America could make him attempt to use anything to eat with besides his hands.

From then on, whenever we mentioned America, he would firmly state that America was "*Apana misuri*" or no good. People there could not eat with their fingers, and they had to put forks into their mouths.

A little while later Dick and Doug had a conversation with Mogo and O'sani.

"Mogo, are you a Mohammedan?" asked Dick.

"H'Apana." (I'm not a Mohammedan.)

"Are you a Christian?"

"No, I'm not a Christian."

"Well then, what are you?"

"Mi-mi grai!" (I am crazy) he laughed.

Then they turned to the other one.

"Say, O'sani," asked Doug, "what's your religion?"

"Bwana, I'm Christian," replied O'sani.

"Why, I thought you were a Mohammedan."

"Yas, Mohammedan, too," came the remarkable reply.

In other words, O'sani was playing on the safe side by being everything at once!

On August the eighth, we moved camp from Serenerra back to Sheltered Valley. This time we entered the valley at the lower end. There was a fair trail for part of the way to the valley which we followed as far as we could. But we soon had to turn off and go across country where there were stones, thorns, and pig holes.

Strange to say, a real pig hole isn't really a pig hole. An ant bear digs the hole at first, then abandons it. The wart hog, who is a lazy fellow, then takes possession. He doesn't live in the hole but uses it as a refuge if he is chased. Consequently the holes are called pig holes. Whether they are dug by a pig or by an ant eater, they are bad things to find in the road of an automobile. It certainly was a wonder to us that we broke no more springs or axles than we did.

A wart hog, incidentally, has a very peculiar way of entering his hole. No matter how close his pursuer is, he always turns and backs down it.

Just as we were entering the valley we saw four young cheetah. This species is a carnivorous animal that looks very much like a leopard. These four were a beautiful sight as they trotted along among the trees. Almost three feet behind each one we could see a black spot travelling along through the grass. We didn't know what this was at first. Then we saw that it was the tip of the animal's tail. The tail of each one was hidden by the grass and only the black tip showed above.

In a short while we came to a little ravine which ran down into the big valley. Our guide, Shai, thought that this was the location of the springs which some Masai had told us about.

So we left the car down in the valley and went up to hunt for water.

It was a beautiful place. The valley was filled with trees and under them long green grass made a soft carpet. On the sides of the hills were bright green trees and bushes. Among the trees were bands of impalla and zebra. A beautiful roan antelope stood under a big mimosa. He watched us a moment, then bounded off up the hill.

Up near the end of the donga, we saw an interesting sight. As we came around a bend we interrupted two little jackals stalking a bunch of monkeys. We had never known that a jackal made kills of his own. These were going about it, though, just as a lion or leopard would stalk a zebra. They were just creeping slowly through the grass toward the unsuspecting monkeys when our coming spoiled it all. As soon as the jackals realized that the monkeys had seen us and were alert, they made a dash for them, hoping to get one before the bunch fled into the trees. But they were unsuccessful. The monkeys gave a scream and scampered into the tall palm trees that grew nearby. There they sat, making faces, first at us, then at the jackals.

For a mile or so, we followed a section of the valley that Mr. and Mrs. Johnson knew. Then suddenly we came into country that was unfamiliar to them. Quickly the valley widened out into a beautiful plain covered with trees. All over the plain were herds of game, giving a wonderful coloring to the scene. There were striped zebra, black wildebeest, pretty little Tommies, impalla whose reddish-brown bodies showed up in a beautiful way against the green background of the trees and thick foliage of the undergrowth.

Just ahead of us and not fifty feet away was a whole herd of impalla, leaping and running for the side of the hill. There was a mature old male with wide spreading horns in front of the herd. Closely following him was his harem of about twenty females. To the right in the hills, a stately herd of eland was grazing in the long thick grass.

Down the slope from us, a bunch of wildebeest were returning from a drink at the waterhole. As we advanced across the plain and into a forest of mimosa and thorn trees dozens of monkeys screamed at us from overhead. Topi and kongoni looked up from their meal of grass. We could see partridge and guinea fowl everywhere. The thickets and bushes along the donga offered perfect cover for lions and leopards. There were a few stretches of tinga-tinga grass that were almost certain to contain buffalo.

From across the donga we heard the barking and yelping of hundreds of zebra. We stopped once near a waterhole to watch a small herd of wildebeest coming down to drink. As they approached, they saw us and stopped with their heads high in the air. They were not much afraid, only cautious.

What a sight it all was! Surely Africa is like a thousand menageries all rolled into one.

Just as we got back to camp and were sitting down for lunch it started to rain. We had noticed the dark clouds gathering in the sky but didn't take them as a serious threat. We decided we would eat lunch even if it poured. As we didn't have a dining tent with us at this camp, we ate right in the open.

In the afternoon Dick and Dave put their bathing suits on to see if they could get a bath in the rain. The boys always laughed at us when we did this. They said, *"Toto grai."* (Meaning crazy boys.) After our baths we went into our tents and got into bed to lead a regular lazy man's life for the rest of the day.

YOUNG DANDIES OF THE MASAI TRIBE.

JUST BEFORE LEAVING NAIROBI FOR HOME.

The rain came down, not in sheets as the saying is, but in blankets and quilts. We never knew it could rain so hard. As there was no shelter anywhere for the boys, the poor fellows crawled under the flaps of our tents, shivering with the cold. In a few minutes, the water began to seep in under Dick's ground cloth. One of the Waccoma boys had ditched Doug's and my tent but had neglected Dick's. So Dick put on his bathing suit again and went out to dig a ditch around his tent. The boys would have done it if Dick had asked them but it seemed unfair to send them out into the cold rain. We had dry clothes to put on but they didn't.

It had rained so hard that there was about an inch of water all over the ground. When Dick began to dig, the water and mud flew all over him. In a minute or two he was so splashed with mud that no one could have recognized him.

After a while Dave saw O'sani button up his ragged coat and start out into the rain. The faithful old fellow was going out to get some supper ready for us. Just then I heard Doug call to him. Doug gave him his poncho. All of us had been equipped at National Scout Headquarters with regulation ponchos. When O'sani put on the rubber poncho he was as happy as a baby with a new toy. He strutted around showing it to the other boys in the tent. Then he went out to the fire and began to get supper. Even after supper was over he stayed out in the wet trying to see just how much rain the poncho would keep off.

All our blankets were in the truck where we had prepared to spend the night. As it was impossible to get our bed clothes into the tent without wetting them in the downpour we spent the night in the truck and let the boys use our tents. They were certainly grateful for this favor.

After getting settled in the truck a Waccoma peeped in through the curtains and asked if he might sleep on the front seat. We said he might and asked him why he didn't sleep in one of the tents. He told us that the boys would not let him. We later found out that he was a "chenzi" or savage to the boys and therefore, by their belief, not fit to sleep under the same shelter with them.

He rolled himself up into the blanket that he wore during the day, and went to sleep. It was curious to see how the natives in the personal service or porter class treated the ordinary natives. The poor savages take all this for granted and are well satisfied with life. As a matter of fact, there was very little difference between the two.

As we were feeling pretty cold and miserable, Doug got up in the middle of the night and made some boiling hot tea.

Next day the rain had driven the game away. For four miles up and down the valley, where we had seen thousands of zebra and wildebeest the day before, we now saw not one head of game.

It is a curious thing about the way rain makes the animals move. They seem to get restless and have an impulse to find new grazing ground. When the rain starts falling whole herds start drifting in one direction and keep in motion until the rain stops. There seems to be no definite idea of getting anywhere but just to move from their present place.

For instance, while all the game had gone from near our camp, when we went down the valley for several miles we found the herds peacefully grazing. The queer thing was that, while the game near camp had moved down, no game had come from up the valley down toward camp. Mr. Johnson said that this was true in all his experiences. The nearby game moved away, but no game moved to where he was.

August 12th was our last day in Sheltered Valley. We got up early so as to have a good start by the time Old Sol rose.

Leaving those hills and animals was like losing our friends. Every animal we saw made us feel sadder. Doug had formed a great affection for the ungainly giraffe. He said that the giraffe's total inability to protect itself gave him a feeling that he could hardly explain.

Then there was the lion. We certainly had no pity for it because of its cruelty to other animals. But, at the same time, we had no dislike. In fact, we rather admired the large cat. When you come to think about it, the lion is not purposely cruel. He kills his victims because it is the only way he knows to furnish himself with food. In most cities thousands of animals are killed every day for food. In the same way the lion must obtain food by the means that nature provides—brute strength.

Many years will pass before we may again look into the eyes of Simba and see the expression of an animal who is not afraid of anything.

As we would not have much time to look

around at Serenerra we felt that in saying good-
bye to Sheltered Valley, we were saying goodbye
to our African adventure. Not wishing to take
any pictures, we just looked around for awhile.
Many of the game that we had become familiar
with showed up that morning. However, they
didn't seem very sorry to see us go.

When we reached camp, we found that the
boys had everything ready for leaving. We got
in the trucks and drove slowly off towards the
Serengetti Plains. On the way we had found
a valley full of game in its natural state, game
that had never been shot at or molested by man.

The last animals we saw as we came out of
the valley onto the veldt were Tommies, their
inquisitive faces turned toward us and little
black tails wagging.

At the Sererra Camp, we spent the early part
of the afternoon packing the thousand and one
things which formed our equipment.

We got under way about 3 P.M. and followed
what we called the Rocky Donga for a few
miles and then turned off and followed one which
ran over back of Rain Hill. Rain Hill was the
home of the eland. We had never gone over
there without seeing a herd. As we left we saw
four eland scarcely a hundred yards in front

of us. By the length of their horns we knew them to be cows.

We visited the same spot where Dick had got his wart hog. The game seemed more friendly than usual, and two young lions that we saw allowed us to get within a few rods of them before they showed any signs of nervousness. They flattened themselves out on the ground and put their heads between their forepaws like playful cats. In this position they sat there and looked at us while we passed within a few feet.

Now that our safari was ended it would perhaps be well to tell of all the game we had seen.

The list begins with what is known as Carnivora, or meat-eaters. In this class (we saw all these animals while in Africa) are: lion, leopard, cheetah, wild cat, and wolf, hyena (spotted), civet cat, mongoose, serval cat.

Next comes the family of dogs, wolves and foxes. Only one of this group was seen—the jackal.

Of the hoofed animals we saw quite a variety, ranging from the small rock rabbit or hyrax, to the buffalo. In this list also are zebra and wart hog.

In the giraffe family, there are only two

members: the giraffe and the okapi. Only three or four okapi have ever been shot by white men in Africa.

The family of antelopes and gazelles is a large one and the most common. Those seen are hartebeeste or kongoni, topi, wildebeest, duiker, klipspringer, crabi, stein buck, dik-dik, waterbuck, reed buck, impalla, Thompson's gazelle or Tommy, Grant's gazelle, roan antelope, bushbuck and eland.

The monkeys are represented by baboons and Sykes monkeys.

Game birds were plentiful and always provided a delicacy on our menus. We saw quail, guinea fowl, sand grouse, bustards, geese, duck, ostrich, storks, pelican, partridge, and various other varieties of water fowl.

Many people will consider that we had seen much game. But when it is considered that there are over one hundred and fifty common kinds, and that we had only seen a few of them, our list does not sound so big.

At dinner that last night, we all drank coffee in order to stay awake as long as possible. We thought that it would be a shame to sleep in the game country without for a last time listening to lions and leopards. The animals seemed to know what we wanted, too, because they roared the whole night and gave us complete satisfaction.

On August 15th we left the Southern Guasho River for Nairobi. On the way we stopped at Narok to report to the District Commissioner. All parties going through must report to him their destination and the purpose of their journey. Here we saw the natives bringing their cattle and sheep down to the waterhole.

After we left Narok, the roads were fairly good. All morning we saw no game. It isn't very plentiful here because it has all been shot out. People often come out here on week-end shooting parties. We had lunch after we had got down into the Kedong Valley.

The scene as we entered the Kedong was one of the most beautiful on our whole trip. All the dongas were covered with lovely green vegetation which had been brought out by the recent rains.

After a stop of a few minutes at Limuru where Mrs. Johnson bought some supplies, we went on to Nairobi. We arrived home at about eight o'clock that night. Two of the trucks came in about ten minutes after us, but the other with the black driver didn't return. Paul, Mogo and

O'sani, who had been in the truck, soon arrived at the house afoot. They said that the truck had a broken spring and was about four miles outside of the town. So Mr. Johnson went back and brought in some supplies. The truck drove up about an hour later.

Mogo, who was supposed to have ridden in Mrs. Johnson's car, had sneaked away and gone with the truck. When Mr. Johnson had heard that the truck had broken down, he said, "Mogo, if you had come in Memsab's car, the truck would not have broken down." Mogo really thought he had made the truck break down.

We were all sorry to get back to Nairobi, for it meant that our safari was over. The journey had been the greatest experience of our lives and a wonderful success from beginning to end. We had had many exciting experiences and some real thrills.

Mrs. Johnson prepared a special dinner that night. She had all the nice things we liked. We ate until we couldn't hold any more.

Then we dreamed happily of the Africa we had enjoyed so much and which we were to leave the next day. And dreamed, too, of the fun of getting home.